SAXON
MATH

Power Up
Workbook

Stephen Hake

Image Credits: (Paper background pieces)   /Shutterstock and donatas1205/
Shutterstock; (bee) unlit/iStock/Getty Image   era daisy, front) rayjunk/Shutterstock;
(gerber daisies, back) Kanea/Shutterstock.

Printed in the U.S.A.

ISBN   978-1-328-49747-5

6 7 8 9 10   0928   26 25 24 23 22 21

4500821647   A B C D E F G

Dear Student,

We enjoy watching the adventures of "Super Heroes" because they have powers that they use for good. Power is the ability to get things done. We acquire power through concentrated effort and practice. We build powerful bodies with vigorous exercise and healthy living. We develop powerful minds by learning and using skills that help us understand the world around us and solve problems that come our way.

We can build our mathematical power in several ways. We can use our memory to store and instantly recall frequently used information. We can improve our ability to solve many kinds of problems mentally without using pencil and paper or a calculator. We can also expand the range of strategies we use to approach and solve new problems.

The Power Up section of each lesson in *Saxon Math Course 1* is designed to build your mathematical power. Each Power Up has three parts: Facts Practice, Mental Math, and Problem Solving. The three parts are printed on every Power Up page where you will record your answers. This workbook contains a Power Up page for every lesson.

Facts Practice is like a race—write the answers as fast as you can without making mistakes. If the information in the Facts Practice is new to you, take time to study the information so that you can recall the facts quickly and can complete the exercise faster next time.

Mental Math is the ability to work with numbers in your head. This skill greatly improves with practice. Each lesson includes several mental math problems. Your teacher will read these to you or ask you to read them in your book. Do your best to find the answer to each problem without using pencil and paper, except to record your answers. Strong mental math ability will help you throughout your life.

Problem Solving is like a puzzle. You need to figure out how to solve each puzzle. There are many different strategies you can use to solve problems. There are also some questions you can ask yourself to better understand a problem and come up with a plan to solve it. Your teacher will guide you through the problem each day. Becoming a good problem solver is a superior skill that is highly rewarded.

The Power Ups will help you excel at math and acquire math power that will serve you well for the rest of your life.

Stephen Hake
Temple City, California

Power Up Workbook

Saxon Math Course 1

Name _____

Power Up Facts	# Possible	Time and Score										
A 40 Addition Facts	40											
B 40 Addition Facts	40											
C 40 Subtraction Facts	40											
D 40 Multiplication Facts	40											
E 40 Multiplication Facts	40											
F 40 Division Facts	40											
G 24 Fractions to Reduce	24											
H 40 Multiplication and Division Facts	40											
I 20 Improper Fractions	20											
J 20 Mixed Numbers	20											
K Metric and Customary Conversions	30											
L Capacity	23											
M Percent-Decimal-Fraction Equivalents	22											
N Measurement Facts	21											

time / # correct

Saxon Math Course 1

Facts   Add.

4 + 6	9 + 9	3 + 4	5 + 5	7 + 8	2 + 3	7 + 0	5 + 9	2 + 6	3 + 9
3 + 5	2 + 2	6 + 7	8 + 8	2 + 9	5 + 7	4 + 9	6 + 6	3 + 8	7 + 7
4 + 4	7 + 9	5 + 8	2 + 7	0 + 0	6 + 8	3 + 7	2 + 4	7 + 1	4 + 8
5 + 6	4 + 7	2 + 5	3 + 6	8 + 9	2 + 8	10 + 10	4 + 5	6 + 9	3 + 3

Mental Math

a.	b.	c.	d.
e.	**f.**	**g.**	**h.**

Problem Solving

Understand

What information am I given?

What am I asked to find or do?

- -

Plan

How can I use the information I am given?

Which strategy should I try?

- -

Solve

Did I follow the plan?

Did I show my work?

Did I write the answer?

- -

Check

Did I use the correct information?

Did I do what was asked?

Is my answer reasonable?

Facts   Add.

4 + 6	9 + 9	3 + 4	5 + 5	7 + 8	2 + 3	7 + 0	5 + 9	2 + 6	3 + 9
3 + 5	2 + 2	6 + 7	8 + 8	2 + 9	5 + 7	4 + 9	6 + 6	3 + 8	7 + 7
4 + 4	7 + 9	5 + 8	2 + 7	0 + 0	6 + 8	3 + 7	2 + 4	7 + 1	4 + 8
5 + 6	4 + 7	2 + 5	3 + 6	8 + 9	2 + 8	10 + 10	4 + 5	6 + 9	3 + 3

Mental Math

a.	**b.**	**c.**	**d.**
e.	**f.**	**g.**	**h.**

Problem Solving

Understand

What information am I given?
What am I asked to find or do?

Plan

How can I use the information I am given?
Which strategy should I try?

Solve

Did I follow the plan?
Did I show my work?
Did I write the answer?

Check

Did I use the correct information?
Did I do what was asked?
Is my answer reasonable?

© Houghton Mifflin Harcourt Publishing Company and Stephen Hake

Facts   Add.

7 + 7	2 + 4	6 + 8	4 + 3	5 + 5	3 + 2	7 + 6	9 + 4	10 + 10	7 + 3
4 + 4	5 + 8	2 + 2	8 + 7	3 + 9	6 + 6	3 + 5	9 + 1	4 + 7	8 + 9
2 + 8	5 + 6	0 + 0	8 + 4	6 + 3	9 + 6	4 + 5	9 + 7	2 + 6	9 + 9
3 + 8	9 + 5	9 + 2	8 + 8	5 + 2	3 + 3	7 + 5	8 + 0	7 + 2	6 + 4

Mental Math

a.	b.	c.	d.
e.	f.	g.	h.

Problem Solving

Understand
What information am I given?
What am I asked to find or do?

Plan
How can I use the information I am given?
Which strategy should I try?

Solve
Did I follow the plan?
Did I show my work?
Did I write the answer?

Check
Did I use the correct information?
Did I do what was asked?
Is my answer reasonable?

Facts   Add.

4 + 6	9 + 9	3 + 4	5 + 5	7 + 8	2 + 3	7 + 0	5 + 9	2 + 6	3 + 9
3 + 5	2 + 2	6 + 7	8 + 8	2 + 9	5 + 7	4 + 9	6 + 6	3 + 8	7 + 7
4 + 4	7 + 9	5 + 8	2 + 7	0 + 0	6 + 8	3 + 7	2 + 4	7 + 1	4 + 8
5 + 6	4 + 7	2 + 5	3 + 6	8 + 9	2 + 8	10 + 10	4 + 5	6 + 9	3 + 3

Mental Math

a.	b.	c.	d.
e.	f.	g.	h.

Problem Solving

Understand

What information am I given?

What am I asked to find or do?

- -

Plan

How can I use the information I am given?

Which strategy should I try?

- -

Solve

Did I follow the plan?

Did I show my work?

Did I write the answer?

- -

Check

Did I use the correct information?

Did I do what was asked?

Is my answer reasonable?

Facts   Add.

7 + 7	2 + 4	6 + 8	4 + 3	5 + 5	3 + 2	7 + 6	9 + 4	10 + 10	7 + 3
4 + 4	5 + 8	2 + 2	8 + 7	3 + 9	6 + 6	3 + 5	9 + 1	4 + 7	8 + 9
2 + 8	5 + 6	0 + 0	8 + 4	6 + 3	9 + 6	4 + 5	9 + 7	2 + 6	9 + 9
3 + 8	9 + 5	9 + 2	8 + 8	5 + 2	3 + 3	7 + 5	8 + 0	7 + 2	6 + 4

Mental Math

a.	b.	c.	d.
e.	f.	g.	h.

Problem Solving

Understand

What information am I given?

What am I asked to find or do?

- -

Plan

How can I use the information I am given?

Which strategy should I try?

- -

Solve

Did I follow the plan?

Did I show my work?

Did I write the answer?

- -

Check

Did I use the correct information?

Did I do what was asked?

Is my answer reasonable?

Facts   Subtract.

8 − 5	10 − 4	12 − 6	6 − 3	8 − 4	14 − 7	20 − 10	11 − 5	7 − 4	13 − 6
7 − 2	15 − 8	9 − 7	17 − 9	10 − 5	8 − 1	16 − 7	6 − 0	12 − 3	9 − 5
13 − 5	11 − 7	14 − 8	10 − 7	5 − 3	15 − 6	6 − 4	10 − 8	18 − 9	15 − 7
12 − 4	11 − 2	16 − 8	9 − 9	13 − 4	11 − 8	9 − 6	14 − 9	8 − 6	12 − 5

Mental Math

a.	b.	c.	d.
e.	f.	g.	h.

Problem Solving

Understand
What information am I given?
What am I asked to find or do?

Plan
How can I use the information I am given?
Which strategy should I try?

Solve
Did I follow the plan?
Did I show my work?
Did I write the answer?

Check
Did I use the correct information?
Did I do what was asked?
Is my answer reasonable?

Facts   Subtract.

8 −5	10 −4	12 −6	6 −3	8 −4	14 −7	20 −10	11 −5	7 −4	13 −6
7 −2	15 −8	9 −7	17 −9	10 −5	8 −1	16 −7	6 −0	12 −3	9 −5
13 −5	11 −7	14 −8	10 −7	5 −3	15 −6	6 −4	10 −8	18 −9	15 −7
12 −4	11 −2	16 −8	9 −9	13 −4	11 −8	9 −6	14 −9	8 −6	12 −5

Mental Math

a.	b.	c.	d.
e.	f.	g.	h.

Problem Solving

Understand

What information am I given?

What am I asked to find or do?

Plan

How can I use the information I am given?

Which strategy should I try?

Solve

Did I follow the plan?

Did I show my work?

Did I write the answer?

Check

Did I use the correct information?

Did I do what was asked?

Is my answer reasonable?

Name _____ Time _____

Facts   Add.

4 + 6	9 + 9	3 + 4	5 + 5	7 + 8	2 + 3	7 + 0	5 + 9	2 + 6	3 + 9
3 + 5	2 + 2	6 + 7	8 + 8	2 + 9	5 + 7	4 + 9	6 + 6	3 + 8	7 + 7
4 + 4	7 + 9	5 + 8	2 + 7	0 + 0	6 + 8	3 + 7	2 + 4	7 + 1	4 + 8
5 + 6	4 + 7	2 + 5	3 + 6	8 + 9	2 + 8	10 + 10	4 + 5	6 + 9	3 + 3

Mental Math

a.	b.	c.	d.
e.	f.	g.	h.

Problem Solving

Understand

What information am I given?

What am I asked to find or do?

Plan

How can I use the information I am given?

Which strategy should I try?

Solve

Did I follow the plan?

Did I show my work?

Did I write the answer?

Check

Did I use the correct information?

Did I do what was asked?

Is my answer reasonable?

Facts   Subtract.

8 − 5	10 − 4	12 − 6	6 − 3	8 − 4	14 − 7	20 − 10	11 − 5	7 − 4	13 − 6
7 − 2	15 − 8	9 − 7	17 − 9	10 − 5	8 − 1	16 − 7	6 − 0	12 − 3	9 − 5
13 − 5	11 − 7	14 − 8	10 − 7	5 − 3	15 − 6	6 − 4	10 − 8	18 − 9	15 − 7
12 − 4	11 − 2	16 − 8	9 − 9	13 − 4	11 − 8	9 − 6	14 − 9	8 − 6	12 − 5

Mental Math

a.	**b.**	**c.**	**d.**
e.	**f.**	**g.**	**h.**

Problem Solving

Understand

What information am I given?

What am I asked to find or do?

Plan

How can I use the information I am given?

Which strategy should I try?

Solve

Did I follow the plan?

Did I show my work?

Did I write the answer?

Check

Did I use the correct information?

Did I do what was asked?

Is my answer reasonable?

Name _____ Time _____

Facts   Subtract.

8 − 5	10 − 4	12 − 6	6 − 3	8 − 4	14 − 7	20 − 10	11 − 5	7 − 4	13 − 6
7 − 2	15 − 8	9 − 7	17 − 9	10 − 5	8 − 1	16 − 7	6 − 0	12 − 3	9 − 5
13 − 5	11 − 7	14 − 8	10 − 7	5 − 3	15 − 6	6 − 4	10 − 8	18 − 9	15 − 7
12 − 4	11 − 2	16 − 8	9 − 9	13 − 4	11 − 8	9 − 6	14 − 9	8 − 6	12 − 5

Mental Math

a.	b.	c.	d.
e.	f.	g.	h.

Problem Solving

Understand

What information am I given?
What am I asked to find or do?

- -

Plan

How can I use the information I am given?
Which strategy should I try?

- -

Solve

Did I follow the plan?
Did I show my work?
Did I write the answer?

- -

Check

Did I use the correct information?
Did I do what was asked?
Is my answer reasonable?

Facts   Multiply.

7 ×7	4 ×6	8 ×1	2 ×2	0 ×5	6 ×3	8 ×9	5 ×8	6 ×2	10 ×10
9 ×4	2 ×5	9 ×6	7 ×3	5 ×5	7 ×2	6 ×8	3 ×5	9 ×9	5 ×4
3 ×4	6 ×5	8 ×2	4 ×4	6 ×7	8 ×8	2 ×3	7 ×4	5 ×9	3 ×8
3 ×9	7 ×8	2 ×4	5 ×7	3 ×3	9 ×7	4 ×8	0 ×0	9 ×2	6 ×6

Mental Math

a.	b.	c.	d.
e.	f.	g.	h.

Problem Solving

Understand

What information am I given?

What am I asked to find or do?

Plan

How can I use the information I am given?

Which strategy should I try?

Solve

Did I follow the plan?

Did I show my work?

Did I write the answer?

Check

Did I use the correct information?

Did I do what was asked?

Is my answer reasonable?

Facts	Multiply.

7 ×7	4 ×6	8 ×1	2 ×2	0 ×5	6 ×3	8 ×9	5 ×8	6 ×2	10 ×10
9 ×4	2 ×5	9 ×6	7 ×3	5 ×5	7 ×2	6 ×8	3 ×5	9 ×9	5 ×4
3 ×4	6 ×5	8 ×2	4 ×4	6 ×7	8 ×8	2 ×3	7 ×4	5 ×9	3 ×8
3 ×9	7 ×8	2 ×4	5 ×7	3 ×3	9 ×7	4 ×8	0 ×0	9 ×2	6 ×6

Mental Math

a.	b.	c.	d.
e.	f.	g.	h.

Problem Solving

Understand
What information am I given?
What am I asked to find or do?

Plan
How can I use the information I am given?
Which strategy should I try?

Solve
Did I follow the plan?
Did I show my work?
Did I write the answer?

Check
Did I use the correct information?
Did I do what was asked?
Is my answer reasonable?

Facts   Add.

4 + 6	9 + 9	3 + 4	5 + 5	7 + 8	2 + 3	7 + 0	5 + 9	2 + 6	3 + 9
3 + 5	2 + 2	6 + 7	8 + 8	2 + 9	5 + 7	4 + 9	6 + 6	3 + 8	7 + 7
4 + 4	7 + 9	5 + 8	2 + 7	0 + 0	6 + 8	3 + 7	2 + 4	7 + 1	4 + 8
5 + 6	4 + 7	2 + 5	3 + 6	8 + 9	2 + 8	10 + 10	4 + 5	6 + 9	3 + 3

Mental Math

a.	b.	c.	d.
e.	f.	g.	h.

Problem Solving

Understand
What information am I given?
What am I asked to find or do?

Plan
How can I use the information I am given?
Which strategy should I try?

Solve
Did I follow the plan?
Did I show my work?
Did I write the answer?

Check
Did I use the correct information?
Did I do what was asked?
Is my answer reasonable?

Facts   Multiply.

7 ×7	4 ×6	8 ×1	2 ×2	0 ×5	6 ×3	8 ×9	5 ×8	6 ×2	10 ×10
9 ×4	2 ×5	9 ×6	7 ×3	5 ×5	7 ×2	6 ×8	3 ×5	9 ×9	5 ×4
3 ×4	6 ×5	8 ×2	4 ×4	6 ×7	8 ×8	2 ×3	7 ×4	5 ×9	3 ×8
3 ×9	7 ×8	2 ×4	5 ×7	3 ×3	9 ×7	4 ×8	0 ×0	9 ×2	6 ×6

Mental Math

a.	b.	c.	d.
e.	f.	g.	h.

Problem Solving

Understand
What information am I given?
What am I asked to find or do?

Plan
How can I use the information I am given?
Which strategy should I try?

Solve
Did I follow the plan?
Did I show my work?
Did I write the answer?

Check
Did I use the correct information?
Did I do what was asked?
Is my answer reasonable?

Facts   Subtract.

8 − 5	10 − 4	12 − 6	6 − 3	8 − 4	14 − 7	20 − 10	11 − 5	7 − 4	13 − 6
7 − 2	15 − 8	9 − 7	17 − 9	10 − 5	8 − 1	16 − 7	6 − 0	12 − 3	9 − 5
13 − 5	11 − 7	14 − 8	10 − 7	5 − 3	15 − 6	6 − 4	10 − 8	18 − 9	15 − 7
12 − 4	11 − 2	16 − 8	9 − 9	13 − 4	11 − 8	9 − 6	14 − 9	8 − 6	12 − 5

Mental Math

a.	b.	c.	d.
e.	f.	g.	h.

Problem Solving

Understand
What information am I given?
What am I asked to find or do?

- -

Plan
How can I use the information I am given?
Which strategy should I try?

- -

Solve
Did I follow the plan?
Did I show my work?
Did I write the answer?

- -

Check
Did I use the correct information?
Did I do what was asked?
Is my answer reasonable?

Facts   Multiply.

7 × 7	4 × 6	8 × 1	2 × 2	0 × 5	6 × 3	8 × 9	5 × 8	6 × 2	10 × 10
9 × 4	2 × 5	9 × 6	7 × 3	5 × 5	7 × 2	6 × 8	3 × 5	9 × 9	5 × 4
3 × 4	6 × 5	8 × 2	4 × 4	6 × 7	8 × 8	2 × 3	7 × 4	5 × 9	3 × 8
3 × 9	7 × 8	2 × 4	5 × 7	3 × 3	9 × 7	4 × 8	0 × 0	9 × 2	6 × 6

Mental Math

a.	b.	c.	d.
e.	f.	g.	h.

Problem Solving

Understand

What information am I given?

What am I asked to find or do?

Plan

How can I use the information I am given?

Which strategy should I try?

Solve

Did I follow the plan?

Did I show my work?

Did I write the answer?

Check

Did I use the correct information?

Did I do what was asked?

Is my answer reasonable?

Name _____ Time _____

Facts Multiply.

8 × 8	3 × 9	6 × 7	5 × 2	0 × 0	3 × 8	4 × 6	5 × 8	2 × 9	9 × 9
6 × 1	2 × 6	3 × 3	4 × 5	5 × 5	8 × 6	4 × 2	7 × 7	7 × 4	5 × 3
6 × 9	8 × 4	5 × 9	4 × 3	7 × 8	2 × 2	6 × 5	2 × 7	8 × 9	3 × 6
4 × 4	5 × 7	3 × 2	7 × 9	6 × 6	3 × 7	2 × 8	0 × 7	9 × 4	10 × 10

Mental Math

a.	b.	c.	d.
e.	f.	g.	h.

Problem Solving

Understand
What information am I given?
What am I asked to find or do?

Plan
How can I use the information I am given?
Which strategy should I try?

Solve
Did I follow the plan?
Did I show my work?
Did I write the answer?

Check
Did I use the correct information?
Did I do what was asked?
Is my answer reasonable?

Name _____ Time _____

Facts   Add.

7 + 7	2 + 4	6 + 8	4 + 3	5 + 5	3 + 2	7 + 6	9 + 4	10 + 10	7 + 3
4 + 4	5 + 8	2 + 2	8 + 7	3 + 9	6 + 6	3 + 5	9 + 1	4 + 7	8 + 9
2 + 8	5 + 6	0 + 0	8 + 4	6 + 3	9 + 6	4 + 5	9 + 7	2 + 6	9 + 9
3 + 8	9 + 5	9 + 2	8 + 8	5 + 2	3 + 3	7 + 5	8 + 0	7 + 2	6 + 4

Mental Math

a.	**b.**	**c.**	**d.**
e.	**f.**	**g.**	**h.**

Problem Solving

Understand

What information am I given?

What am I asked to find or do?

- -

Plan

How can I use the information I am given?

Which strategy should I try?

- -

Solve

Did I follow the plan?

Did I show my work?

Did I write the answer?

- -

Check

Did I use the correct information?

Did I do what was asked?

Is my answer reasonable?

Facts	Multiply.								

7 ×7	4 ×6	8 ×1	2 ×2	0 ×5	6 ×3	8 ×9	5 ×8	6 ×2	10 ×10
9 ×4	2 ×5	9 ×6	7 ×3	5 ×5	7 ×2	6 ×8	3 ×5	9 ×9	5 ×4
3 ×4	6 ×5	8 ×2	4 ×4	6 ×7	8 ×8	2 ×3	7 ×4	5 ×9	3 ×8
3 ×9	7 ×8	2 ×4	5 ×7	3 ×3	9 ×7	4 ×8	0 ×0	9 ×2	6 ×6

Mental Math

a.	b.	c.	d.
e.	f.	g.	h.

Problem Solving

Understand
What information am I given?
What am I asked to find or do?

Plan
How can I use the information I am given?
Which strategy should I try?

Solve
Did I follow the plan?
Did I show my work?
Did I write the answer?

Check
Did I use the correct information?
Did I do what was asked?
Is my answer reasonable?

Facts   Subtract.

8 −5	10 − 4	12 − 6	6 −3	8 −4	14 − 7	20 −10	11 − 5	7 −4	13 − 6
7 −2	15 − 8	9 − 7	17 − 9	10 − 5	8 −1	16 − 7	6 −0	12 − 3	9 −5
13 − 5	11 − 7	14 − 8	10 − 7	5 −3	15 − 6	6 −4	10 − 8	18 − 9	15 − 7
12 − 4	11 − 2	16 − 8	9 −9	13 − 4	11 − 8	9 −6	14 − 9	8 −6	12 − 5

Mental Math

a.	b.	c.	d.
e.	f.	g.	h.

Problem Solving

Understand

What information am I given?
What am I asked to find or do?

Plan

How can I use the information I am given?
Which strategy should I try?

Solve

Did I follow the plan?
Did I show my work?
Did I write the answer?

Check

Did I use the correct information?
Did I do what was asked?
Is my answer reasonable?

Facts Multiply.

7 × 7	4 × 6	8 × 1	2 × 2	0 × 5	6 × 3	8 × 9	5 × 8	6 × 2	10 × 10
9 × 4	2 × 5	9 × 6	7 × 3	5 × 5	7 × 2	6 × 8	3 × 5	9 × 9	5 × 4
3 × 4	6 × 5	8 × 2	4 × 4	6 × 7	8 × 8	2 × 3	7 × 4	5 × 9	3 × 8
3 × 9	7 × 8	2 × 4	5 × 7	3 × 3	9 × 7	4 × 8	0 × 0	9 × 2	6 × 6

Mental Math

a.	**b.**	**c.**	**d.**
e.	**f.**	**g.**	**h.**

Problem Solving

Understand
What information am I given?
What am I asked to find or do?

- -

Plan
How can I use the information I am given?
Which strategy should I try?

- -

Solve
Did I follow the plan?
Did I show my work?
Did I write the answer?

- -

Check
Did I use the correct information?
Did I do what was asked?
Is my answer reasonable?

Facts   Subtract.

8 − 5	10 − 4	12 − 6	6 − 3	8 − 4	14 − 7	20 − 10	11 − 5	7 − 4	13 − 6
7 − 2	15 − 8	9 − 7	17 − 9	10 − 5	8 − 1	16 − 7	6 − 0	12 − 3	9 − 5
13 − 5	11 − 7	14 − 8	10 − 7	5 − 3	15 − 6	6 − 4	10 − 8	18 − 9	15 − 7
12 − 4	11 − 2	16 − 8	9 − 9	13 − 4	11 − 8	9 − 6	14 − 9	8 − 6	12 − 5

Mental Math

a.	b.	c.	d.
e.	f.	g.	h.

Problem Solving

Understand
What information am I given?
What am I asked to find or do?

- -

Plan
How can I use the information I am given?
Which strategy should I try?

- -

Solve
Did I follow the plan?
Did I show my work?
Did I write the answer?

- -

Check
Did I use the correct information?
Did I do what was asked?
Is my answer reasonable?

| Facts | Multiply. |

7 × 7	4 × 6	8 × 1	2 × 2	0 × 5	6 × 3	8 × 9	5 × 8	6 × 2	10 × 10
9 × 4	2 × 5	9 × 6	7 × 3	5 × 5	7 × 2	6 × 8	3 × 5	9 × 9	5 × 4
3 × 4	6 × 5	8 × 2	4 × 4	6 × 7	8 × 8	2 × 3	7 × 4	5 × 9	3 × 8
3 × 9	7 × 8	2 × 4	5 × 7	3 × 3	9 × 7	4 × 8	0 × 0	9 × 2	6 × 6

Mental Math

a.	b.	c.	d.
e.	f.	g.	h.

Problem Solving

Understand

What information am I given?
What am I asked to find or do?

- -

Plan

How can I use the information I am given?
Which strategy should I try?

- -

Solve

Did I follow the plan?
Did I show my work?
Did I write the answer?

- -

Check

Did I use the correct information?
Did I do what was asked?
Is my answer reasonable?

Facts Subtract.

8 −5	10 − 4	12 − 6	6 −3	8 −4	14 − 7	20 −10	11 − 5	7 −4	13 − 6
7 −2	15 − 8	9 − 7	17 − 9	10 − 5	8 −1	16 − 7	6 −0	12 − 3	9 −5
13 − 5	11 − 7	14 − 8	10 − 7	5 −3	15 − 6	6 −4	10 − 8	18 − 9	15 − 7
12 − 4	11 − 2	16 − 8	9 −9	13 − 4	11 − 8	9 −6	14 − 9	8 − 6	12 − 5

Mental Math

a.	b.	c.	d.
e.	f.	g.	h.

Problem Solving

Understand

What information am I given?

What am I asked to find or do?

- -

Plan

How can I use the information I am given?

Which strategy should I try?

- -

Solve

Did I follow the plan?

Did I show my work?

Did I write the answer?

- -

Check

Did I use the correct information?

Did I do what was asked?

Is my answer reasonable?

Facts	Divide.								
7)49	9)27	5)25	4)12	6)36	7)21	10)100	5)10	4)0	4)16
8)72	4)28	2)14	7)35	5)40	2)8	8)8	3)9	8)24	4)24
6)54	3)18	8)56	3)6	8)48	5)20	2)16	7)63	6)12	1)6
4)32	9)45	2)18	8)64	6)30	5)15	6)42	3)24	9)81	4)36

Mental Math

a.	b.	c.	d.
e.	f.	g.	h.

Problem Solving

Understand

What information am I given?
What am I asked to find or do?

Plan

How can I use the information I am given?
Which strategy should I try?

Solve

Did I follow the plan?
Did I show my work?
Did I write the answer?

Check

Did I use the correct information?
Did I do what was asked?
Is my answer reasonable?

Facts   Subtract.

8 − 5	10 − 4	12 − 6	6 − 3	8 − 4	14 − 7	20 −10	11 − 5	7 − 4	13 − 6
7 − 2	15 − 8	9 − 7	17 − 9	10 − 5	8 − 1	16 − 7	6 − 0	12 − 3	9 − 5
13 − 5	11 − 7	14 − 8	10 − 7	5 − 3	15 − 6	6 − 4	10 − 8	18 − 9	15 − 7
12 − 4	11 − 2	16 − 8	9 − 9	13 − 4	11 − 8	9 − 6	14 − 9	8 − 6	12 − 5

Mental Math

a.	**b.**	**c.**	**d.**
e.	**f.**	**g.**	**h.**

Problem Solving

Understand

What information am I given?

What am I asked to find or do?

- -

Plan

How can I use the information I am given?

Which strategy should I try?

- -

Solve

Did I follow the plan?

Did I show my work?

Did I write the answer?

- -

Check

Did I use the correct information?

Did I do what was asked?

Is my answer reasonable?

Facts   Multiply.

8 × 8	3 × 9	6 × 7	5 × 2	0 × 0	3 × 8	4 × 6	5 × 8	2 × 9	9 × 9
6 × 1	2 × 6	3 × 3	4 × 5	5 × 5	8 × 6	4 × 2	7 × 7	7 × 4	5 × 3
6 × 9	8 × 4	5 × 9	4 × 3	7 × 8	2 × 2	6 × 5	2 × 7	8 × 9	3 × 6
4 × 4	5 × 7	3 × 2	7 × 9	6 × 6	3 × 7	2 × 8	0 × 7	9 × 4	10 × 10

Mental Math

a.	b.	c.	d.
e.	f.	g.	h.

Problem Solving

Understand

What information am I given?
What am I asked to find or do?

Plan

How can I use the information I am given?
Which strategy should I try?

Solve

Did I follow the plan?
Did I show my work?
Did I write the answer?

Check

Did I use the correct information?
Did I do what was asked?
Is my answer reasonable?

Name _____ Time _____

Facts   Divide.

7)49	9)27	5)25	4)12	6)36	7)21	10)100	5)10	4)0	4)16
8)72	4)28	2)14	7)35	5)40	2)8	8)8	3)9	8)24	4)24
6)54	3)18	8)56	3)6	8)48	5)20	2)16	7)63	6)12	1)6
4)32	9)45	2)18	8)64	6)30	5)15	6)42	3)24	9)81	4)36

Mental Math

a.	**b.**	**c.**	**d.**
e.	**f.**	**g.**	**h.**

Problem Solving

Understand

What information am I given?

What am I asked to find or do?

- -

Plan

How can I use the information I am given?

Which strategy should I try?

- -

Solve

Did I follow the plan?

Did I show my work?

Did I write the answer?

- -

Check

Did I use the correct information?

Did I do what was asked?

Is my answer reasonable?

Facts   Add.

7 + 7	2 + 4	6 + 8	4 + 3	5 + 5	3 + 2	7 + 6	9 + 4	10 + 10	7 + 3
4 + 4	5 + 8	2 + 2	8 + 7	3 + 9	6 + 6	3 + 5	9 + 1	4 + 7	8 + 9
2 + 8	5 + 6	0 + 0	8 + 4	6 + 3	9 + 6	4 + 5	9 + 7	2 + 6	9 + 9
3 + 8	9 + 5	9 + 2	8 + 8	5 + 2	3 + 3	7 + 5	8 + 0	7 + 2	6 + 4

Mental Math

a.	b.	c.	d.
e.	f.	g.	h.

Problem Solving

Understand

What information am I given?
What am I asked to find or do?

Plan

How can I use the information I am given?
Which strategy should I try?

Solve

Did I follow the plan?
Did I show my work?
Did I write the answer?

Check

Did I use the correct information?
Did I do what was asked?
Is my answer reasonable?

Facts Multiply.

8 × 8	3 × 9	6 × 7	5 × 2	0 × 0	3 × 8	4 × 6	5 × 8	2 × 9	9 × 9
6 × 1	2 × 6	3 × 3	4 × 5	5 × 5	8 × 6	4 × 2	7 × 7	7 × 4	5 × 3
6 × 9	8 × 4	5 × 9	4 × 3	7 × 8	2 × 2	6 × 5	2 × 7	8 × 9	3 × 6
4 × 4	5 × 7	3 × 2	7 × 9	6 × 6	3 × 7	2 × 8	0 × 7	9 × 4	10 × 10

Mental Math

a.	b.	c.	d.
e.	f.	g.	h.

Problem Solving

Understand

What information am I given?

What am I asked to find or do?

- -

Plan

How can I use the information I am given?

Which strategy should I try?

- -

Solve

Did I follow the plan?

Did I show my work?

Did I write the answer?

- -

Check

Did I use the correct information?

Did I do what was asked?

Is my answer reasonable?

Facts   Divide.

7)49	9)27	5)25	4)12	6)36	7)21	10)100	5)10	4)0	4)16
8)72	4)28	2)14	7)35	5)40	2)8	8)8	3)9	8)24	4)24
6)54	3)18	8)56	3)6	8)48	5)20	2)16	7)63	6)12	1)6
4)32	9)45	2)18	8)64	6)30	5)15	6)42	3)24	9)81	4)36

Mental Math

a.	**b.**	**c.**	**d.**
e.	**f.**	**g.**	**h.**

Problem Solving

Understand

What information am I given?
What am I asked to find or do?

- -

Plan

How can I use the information I am given?
Which strategy should I try?

- -

Solve

Did I follow the plan?
Did I show my work?
Did I write the answer?

- -

Check

Did I use the correct information?
Did I do what was asked?
Is my answer reasonable?

Facts — Reduce each fraction to lowest terms.

$\frac{2}{8} =$	$\frac{4}{6} =$	$\frac{6}{10} =$	$\frac{2}{4} =$	$\frac{5}{100} =$	$\frac{9}{12} =$
$\frac{4}{10} =$	$\frac{4}{12} =$	$\frac{2}{10} =$	$\frac{3}{6} =$	$\frac{25}{100} =$	$\frac{3}{12} =$
$\frac{4}{16} =$	$\frac{3}{9} =$	$\frac{6}{9} =$	$\frac{4}{8} =$	$\frac{2}{12} =$	$\frac{6}{12} =$
$\frac{8}{16} =$	$\frac{2}{6} =$	$\frac{8}{12} =$	$\frac{6}{8} =$	$\frac{5}{10} =$	$\frac{75}{100} =$

Mental Math

a.	b.	c.	d.
e.	f.	g.	h.

Problem Solving

Understand

What information am I given?

What am I asked to find or do?

Plan

How can I use the information I am given?

Which strategy should I try?

Solve

Did I follow the plan?

Did I show my work?

Did I write the answer?

Check

Did I use the correct information?

Did I do what was asked?

Is my answer reasonable?

Facts — Reduce each fraction to lowest terms.

$\frac{2}{8}$ =	$\frac{4}{6}$ =	$\frac{6}{10}$ =	$\frac{2}{4}$ =	$\frac{5}{100}$ =	$\frac{9}{12}$ =
$\frac{4}{10}$ =	$\frac{4}{12}$ =	$\frac{2}{10}$ =	$\frac{3}{6}$ =	$\frac{25}{100}$ =	$\frac{3}{12}$ =
$\frac{4}{16}$ =	$\frac{3}{9}$ =	$\frac{6}{9}$ =	$\frac{4}{8}$ =	$\frac{2}{12}$ =	$\frac{6}{12}$ =
$\frac{8}{16}$ =	$\frac{2}{6}$ =	$\frac{8}{12}$ =	$\frac{6}{8}$ =	$\frac{5}{10}$ =	$\frac{75}{100}$ =

Mental Math

a.	**b.**	**c.**	**d.**
e.	**f.**	**g.**	**h.**

Problem Solving

Understand

What information am I given?

What am I asked to find or do?

Plan

How can I use the information I am given?

Which strategy should I try?

Solve

Did I follow the plan?

Did I show my work?

Did I write the answer?

Check

Did I use the correct information?

Did I do what was asked?

Is my answer reasonable?

Facts   Multiply.

7 × 7	4 × 6	8 × 1	2 × 2	0 × 5	6 × 3	8 × 9	5 × 8	6 × 2	10 × 10
9 × 4	2 × 5	9 × 6	7 × 3	5 × 5	7 × 2	6 × 8	3 × 5	9 × 9	5 × 4
3 × 4	6 × 5	8 × 2	4 × 4	6 × 7	8 × 8	2 × 3	7 × 4	5 × 9	3 × 8
3 × 9	7 × 8	2 × 4	5 × 7	3 × 3	9 × 7	4 × 8	0 × 0	9 × 2	6 × 6

Mental Math

a.	**b.**	**c.**	**d.**
e.	**f.**	**g.**	**h.**

Problem Solving

Understand

What information am I given?
What am I asked to find or do?

Plan

How can I use the information I am given?
Which strategy should I try?

Solve

Did I follow the plan?
Did I show my work?
Did I write the answer?

Check

Did I use the correct information?
Did I do what was asked?
Is my answer reasonable?

Saxon Math Course 1

Facts Reduce each fraction to lowest terms.

$\frac{2}{8} =$	$\frac{4}{6} =$	$\frac{6}{10} =$	$\frac{2}{4} =$	$\frac{5}{100} =$	$\frac{9}{12} =$
$\frac{4}{10} =$	$\frac{4}{12} =$	$\frac{2}{10} =$	$\frac{3}{6} =$	$\frac{25}{100} =$	$\frac{3}{12} =$
$\frac{4}{16} =$	$\frac{3}{9} =$	$\frac{6}{9} =$	$\frac{4}{8} =$	$\frac{2}{12} =$	$\frac{6}{12} =$
$\frac{8}{16} =$	$\frac{2}{6} =$	$\frac{8}{12} =$	$\frac{6}{8} =$	$\frac{5}{10} =$	$\frac{75}{100} =$

Mental Math

a.	**b.**	**c.**	**d.**
e.	**f.**	**g.**	**h.**

Problem Solving

Understand
What information am I given?
What am I asked to find or do?

- -

Plan
How can I use the information I am given?
Which strategy should I try?

- -

Solve
Did I follow the plan?
Did I show my work?
Did I write the answer?

- -

Check
Did I use the correct information?
Did I do what was asked?
Is my answer reasonable?

Facts   Divide.

$7\overline{)49}$	$9\overline{)27}$	$5\overline{)25}$	$4\overline{)12}$	$6\overline{)36}$	$7\overline{)21}$	$10\overline{)100}$	$5\overline{)10}$	$4\overline{)0}$	$4\overline{)16}$
$8\overline{)72}$	$4\overline{)28}$	$2\overline{)14}$	$7\overline{)35}$	$5\overline{)40}$	$2\overline{)8}$	$8\overline{)8}$	$3\overline{)9}$	$8\overline{)24}$	$4\overline{)24}$
$6\overline{)54}$	$3\overline{)18}$	$8\overline{)56}$	$3\overline{)6}$	$8\overline{)48}$	$5\overline{)20}$	$2\overline{)16}$	$7\overline{)63}$	$6\overline{)12}$	$1\overline{)6}$
$4\overline{)32}$	$9\overline{)45}$	$2\overline{)18}$	$8\overline{)64}$	$6\overline{)30}$	$5\overline{)15}$	$6\overline{)42}$	$3\overline{)24}$	$9\overline{)81}$	$4\overline{)36}$

Mental Math

a.	**b.**	**c.**	**d.**
e.	**f.**	**g.**	**h.**

Problem Solving

Understand

What information am I given?

What am I asked to find or do?

- -

Plan

How can I use the information I am given?

Which strategy should I try?

- -

Solve

Did I follow the plan?

Did I show my work?

Did I write the answer?

- -

Check

Did I use the correct information?

Did I do what was asked?

Is my answer reasonable?

Facts   Reduce each fraction to lowest terms.

$\dfrac{2}{8} =$	$\dfrac{4}{6} =$	$\dfrac{6}{10} =$	$\dfrac{2}{4} =$	$\dfrac{5}{100} =$	$\dfrac{9}{12} =$
$\dfrac{4}{10} =$	$\dfrac{4}{12} =$	$\dfrac{2}{10} =$	$\dfrac{3}{6} =$	$\dfrac{25}{100} =$	$\dfrac{3}{12} =$
$\dfrac{4}{16} =$	$\dfrac{3}{9} =$	$\dfrac{6}{9} =$	$\dfrac{4}{8} =$	$\dfrac{2}{12} =$	$\dfrac{6}{12} =$
$\dfrac{8}{16} =$	$\dfrac{2}{6} =$	$\dfrac{8}{12} =$	$\dfrac{6}{8} =$	$\dfrac{5}{10} =$	$\dfrac{75}{100} =$

Mental Math

a.	**b.**	**c.**	**d.**
e.	**f.**	**g.**	**h.**

Problem Solving

Understand
What information am I given?
What am I asked to find or do?

- -

Plan
How can I use the information I am given?
Which strategy should I try?

- -

Solve
Did I follow the plan?
Did I show my work?
Did I write the answer?

- -

Check
Did I use the correct information?
Did I do what was asked?
Is my answer reasonable?

Facts Add.

4 + 6	9 + 9	3 + 4	5 + 5	7 + 8	2 + 3	7 + 0	5 + 9	2 + 6	3 + 9
3 + 5	2 + 2	6 + 7	8 + 8	2 + 9	5 + 7	4 + 9	6 + 6	3 + 8	7 + 7
4 + 4	7 + 9	5 + 8	2 + 7	0 + 0	6 + 8	3 + 7	2 + 4	7 + 1	4 + 8
5 + 6	4 + 7	2 + 5	3 + 6	8 + 9	2 + 8	10 + 10	4 + 5	6 + 9	3 + 3

Mental Math

a.	**b.**	**c.**	**d.**
e.	**f.**	**g.**	**h.**

Problem Solving

Understand

What information am I given?
What am I asked to find or do?

Plan

How can I use the information I am given?
Which strategy should I try?

Solve

Did I follow the plan?
Did I show my work?
Did I write the answer?

Check

Did I use the correct information?
Did I do what was asked?
Is my answer reasonable?

Facts   Reduce each fraction to lowest terms.

$\frac{2}{8}$ =	$\frac{4}{6}$ =	$\frac{6}{10}$ =	$\frac{2}{4}$ =	$\frac{5}{100}$ =	$\frac{9}{12}$ =
$\frac{4}{10}$ =	$\frac{4}{12}$ =	$\frac{2}{10}$ =	$\frac{3}{6}$ =	$\frac{25}{100}$ =	$\frac{3}{12}$ =
$\frac{4}{16}$ =	$\frac{3}{9}$ =	$\frac{6}{9}$ =	$\frac{4}{8}$ =	$\frac{2}{12}$ =	$\frac{6}{12}$ =
$\frac{8}{16}$ =	$\frac{2}{6}$ =	$\frac{8}{12}$ =	$\frac{6}{8}$ =	$\frac{5}{10}$ =	$\frac{75}{100}$ =

Mental Math

a.	**b.**	**c.**	**d.**
e.	**f.**	**g.**	**h.**

Problem Solving

Understand

What information am I given?

What am I asked to find or do?

- -

Plan

How can I use the information I am given?

Which strategy should I try?

- -

Solve

Did I follow the plan?

Did I show my work?

Did I write the answer?

- -

Check

Did I use the correct information?

Did I do what was asked?

Is my answer reasonable?

Facts	Multiply.								
7 $\times 7$	4 $\times 6$	8 $\times 1$	2 $\times 2$	0 $\times 5$	6 $\times 3$	8 $\times 9$	5 $\times 8$	6 $\times 2$	10 $\times 10$
9 $\times 4$	2 $\times 5$	9 $\times 6$	7 $\times 3$	5 $\times 5$	7 $\times 2$	6 $\times 8$	3 $\times 5$	9 $\times 9$	5 $\times 4$
3 $\times 4$	6 $\times 5$	8 $\times 2$	4 $\times 4$	6 $\times 7$	8 $\times 8$	2 $\times 3$	7 $\times 4$	5 $\times 9$	3 $\times 8$
3 $\times 9$	7 $\times 8$	2 $\times 4$	5 $\times 7$	3 $\times 3$	9 $\times 7$	4 $\times 8$	0 $\times 0$	9 $\times 2$	6 $\times 6$

Mental Math			
a.	**b.**	**c.**	**d.**
e.	**f.**	**g.**	**h.**

Problem Solving

Understand

What information am I given?
What am I asked to find or do?

- -

Plan

How can I use the information I am given?
Which strategy should I try?

- -

Solve

Did I follow the plan?
Did I show my work?
Did I write the answer?

- -

Check

Did I use the correct information?
Did I do what was asked?
Is my answer reasonable?

| Facts | Reduce each fraction to lowest terms. |
</br>

$\frac{2}{8} =$	$\frac{4}{6} =$	$\frac{6}{10} =$	$\frac{2}{4} =$	$\frac{5}{100} =$	$\frac{9}{12} =$
$\frac{4}{10} =$	$\frac{4}{12} =$	$\frac{2}{10} =$	$\frac{3}{6} =$	$\frac{25}{100} =$	$\frac{3}{12} =$
$\frac{4}{16} =$	$\frac{3}{9} =$	$\frac{6}{9} =$	$\frac{4}{8} =$	$\frac{2}{12} =$	$\frac{6}{12} =$
$\frac{8}{16} =$	$\frac{2}{6} =$	$\frac{8}{12} =$	$\frac{6}{8} =$	$\frac{5}{10} =$	$\frac{75}{100} =$

Mental Math

a.	b.	c.	d.
e.	f.	g.	h.

Problem Solving

Understand

What information am I given?
What am I asked to find or do?

- -

Plan

How can I use the information I am given?
Which strategy should I try?

- -

Solve

Did I follow the plan?
Did I show my work?
Did I write the answer?

- -

Check

Did I use the correct information?
Did I do what was asked?
Is my answer reasonable?

| Facts | Reduce each fraction to lowest terms. |

$\frac{2}{8}$ =	$\frac{4}{6}$ =	$\frac{6}{10}$ =	$\frac{2}{4}$ =	$\frac{5}{100}$ =	$\frac{9}{12}$ =
$\frac{4}{10}$ =	$\frac{4}{12}$ =	$\frac{2}{10}$ =	$\frac{3}{6}$ =	$\frac{25}{100}$ =	$\frac{3}{12}$ =
$\frac{4}{16}$ =	$\frac{3}{9}$ =	$\frac{6}{9}$ =	$\frac{4}{8}$ =	$\frac{2}{12}$ =	$\frac{6}{12}$ =
$\frac{8}{16}$ =	$\frac{2}{6}$ =	$\frac{8}{12}$ =	$\frac{6}{8}$ =	$\frac{5}{10}$ =	$\frac{75}{100}$ =

Mental Math

a.	b.	c.	d.
e.	f.	g.	h.

Problem Solving

Understand

What information am I given?
What am I asked to find or do?

- -

Plan

How can I use the information I am given?
Which strategy should I try?

- -

Solve

Did I follow the plan?
Did I show my work?
Did I write the answer?

- -

Check

Did I use the correct information?
Did I do what was asked?
Is my answer reasonable?

Facts   Subtract.

8 − 5	10 − 4	12 − 6	6 − 3	8 − 4	14 − 7	20 − 10	11 − 5	7 − 4	13 − 6
7 − 2	15 − 8	9 − 7	17 − 9	10 − 5	8 − 1	16 − 7	6 − 0	12 − 3	9 − 5
13 − 5	11 − 7	14 − 8	10 − 7	5 − 3	15 − 6	6 − 4	10 − 8	18 − 9	15 − 7
12 − 4	11 − 2	16 − 8	9 − 9	13 − 4	11 − 8	9 − 6	14 − 9	8 − 6	12 − 5

Mental Math

a.	b.	c.	d.
e.	f.	g.	h.

Problem Solving

Understand
What information am I given?
What am I asked to find or do?

Plan
How can I use the information I am given?
Which strategy should I try?

Solve
Did I follow the plan?
Did I show my work?
Did I write the answer?

Check
Did I use the correct information?
Did I do what was asked?
Is my answer reasonable?

Facts   Reduce each fraction to lowest terms.

$\frac{2}{8}$ =	$\frac{4}{6}$ =	$\frac{6}{10}$ =	$\frac{2}{4}$ =	$\frac{5}{100}$ =	$\frac{9}{12}$ =
$\frac{4}{10}$ =	$\frac{4}{12}$ =	$\frac{2}{10}$ =	$\frac{3}{6}$ =	$\frac{25}{100}$ =	$\frac{3}{12}$ =
$\frac{4}{16}$ =	$\frac{3}{9}$ =	$\frac{6}{9}$ =	$\frac{4}{8}$ =	$\frac{2}{12}$ =	$\frac{6}{12}$ =
$\frac{8}{16}$ =	$\frac{2}{6}$ =	$\frac{8}{12}$ =	$\frac{6}{8}$ =	$\frac{5}{10}$ =	$\frac{75}{100}$ =

Mental Math

a.	**b.**	**c.**	**d.**
e.	**f.**	**g.**	**h.**

Problem Solving

Understand
What information am I given?
What am I asked to find or do?

Plan
How can I use the information I am given?
Which strategy should I try?

Solve
Did I follow the plan?
Did I show my work?
Did I write the answer?

Check
Did I use the correct information?
Did I do what was asked?
Is my answer reasonable?

Facts Divide.

7)49	9)27	5)25	4)12	6)36	7)21	10)100	5)10	4)0	4)16
8)72	4)28	2)14	7)35	5)40	2)8	8)8	3)9	8)24	4)24
6)54	3)18	8)56	3)6	8)48	5)20	2)16	7)63	6)12	1)6
4)32	9)45	2)18	8)64	6)30	5)15	6)42	3)24	9)81	4)36

Mental Math

a.	**b.**	**c.**	**d.**
e.	**f.**	**g.**	**h.**

Problem Solving

Understand

What information am I given?
What am I asked to find or do?

- -

Plan

How can I use the information I am given?
Which strategy should I try?

- -

Solve

Did I follow the plan?
Did I show my work?
Did I write the answer?

- -

Check

Did I use the correct information?
Did I do what was asked?
Is my answer reasonable?

Facts   Reduce each fraction to lowest terms.

$\frac{2}{8}$ =	$\frac{4}{6}$ =	$\frac{6}{10}$ =	$\frac{2}{4}$ =	$\frac{5}{100}$ =	$\frac{9}{12}$ =
$\frac{4}{10}$ =	$\frac{4}{12}$ =	$\frac{2}{10}$ =	$\frac{3}{6}$ =	$\frac{25}{100}$ =	$\frac{3}{12}$ =
$\frac{4}{16}$ =	$\frac{3}{9}$ =	$\frac{6}{9}$ =	$\frac{4}{8}$ =	$\frac{2}{12}$ =	$\frac{6}{12}$ =
$\frac{8}{16}$ =	$\frac{2}{6}$ =	$\frac{8}{12}$ =	$\frac{6}{8}$ =	$\frac{5}{10}$ =	$\frac{75}{100}$ =

Mental Math

a.	**b.**	**c.**	**d.**
e.	**f.**	**g.**	**h.**

Problem Solving

Understand

What information am I given?

What am I asked to find or do?

Plan

How can I use the information I am given?

Which strategy should I try?

Solve

Did I follow the plan?

Did I show my work?

Did I write the answer?

Check

Did I use the correct information?

Did I do what was asked?

Is my answer reasonable?

Facts   Multiply.

8 × 8	3 × 9	6 × 7	5 × 2	0 × 0	3 × 8	4 × 6	5 × 8	2 × 9	9 × 9
6 × 1	2 × 6	3 × 3	4 × 5	5 × 5	8 × 6	4 × 2	7 × 7	7 × 4	5 × 3
6 × 9	8 × 4	5 × 9	4 × 3	7 × 8	2 × 2	6 × 5	2 × 7	8 × 9	3 × 6
4 × 4	5 × 7	3 × 2	7 × 9	6 × 6	3 × 7	2 × 8	0 × 7	9 × 4	10 × 10

Mental Math

a.	b.	c.	d.
e.	f.	g.	h.

Problem Solving

Understand

What information am I given?

What am I asked to find or do?

- -

Plan

How can I use the information I am given?

Which strategy should I try?

- -

Solve

Did I follow the plan?

Did I show my work?

Did I write the answer?

- -

Check

Did I use the correct information?

Did I do what was asked?

Is my answer reasonable?

Facts — Reduce each fraction to lowest terms.

$\frac{2}{8}$ =	$\frac{4}{6}$ =	$\frac{6}{10}$ =	$\frac{2}{4}$ =	$\frac{5}{100}$ =	$\frac{9}{12}$ =
$\frac{4}{10}$ =	$\frac{4}{12}$ =	$\frac{2}{10}$ =	$\frac{3}{6}$ =	$\frac{25}{100}$ =	$\frac{3}{12}$ =
$\frac{4}{16}$ =	$\frac{3}{9}$ =	$\frac{6}{9}$ =	$\frac{4}{8}$ =	$\frac{2}{12}$ =	$\frac{6}{12}$ =
$\frac{8}{16}$ =	$\frac{2}{6}$ =	$\frac{8}{12}$ =	$\frac{6}{8}$ =	$\frac{5}{10}$ =	$\frac{75}{100}$ =

Mental Math

a.	**b.**	**c.**	**d.**
e.	**f.**	**g.**	**h.**

Problem Solving

Understand

What information am I given?
What am I asked to find or do?

Plan

How can I use the information I am given?
Which strategy should I try?

Solve

Did I follow the plan?
Did I show my work?
Did I write the answer?

Check

Did I use the correct information?
Did I do what was asked?
Is my answer reasonable?

Facts   Multiply or divide as indicated.

4 × 9	4)‾16	6 × 8	3)‾12	5 × 7	4)‾32	3 × 9	9)‾81	6 × 2	8)‾64
9 × 7	8)‾40	2 × 4	6)‾42	5 × 5	7)‾14	7 × 7	8)‾8	3 × 3	6)‾0
7 × 3	2)‾10	10 × 10	3)‾24	4 × 5	9)‾54	9 × 1	3)‾6	7 × 4	7)‾56
6 × 6	2)‾18	3 × 5	5)‾30	2 × 2	6)‾18	9 × 5	6)‾24	2 × 8	9)‾72

Mental Math

a.	b.	c.	d.
e.	**f.**	**g.**	**h.**

Problem Solving

Understand

What information am I given?

What am I asked to find or do?

- -

Plan

How can I use the information I am given?

Which strategy should I try?

- -

Solve

Did I follow the plan?

Did I show my work?

Did I write the answer?

- -

Check

Did I use the correct information?

Did I do what was asked?

Is my answer reasonable?

Facts   Reduce each fraction to lowest terms.

$\frac{2}{8}$ =	$\frac{4}{6}$ =	$\frac{6}{10}$ =	$\frac{2}{4}$ =	$\frac{5}{100}$ =	$\frac{9}{12}$ =
$\frac{4}{10}$ =	$\frac{4}{12}$ =	$\frac{2}{10}$ =	$\frac{3}{6}$ =	$\frac{25}{100}$ =	$\frac{3}{12}$ =
$\frac{4}{16}$ =	$\frac{3}{9}$ =	$\frac{6}{9}$ =	$\frac{4}{8}$ =	$\frac{2}{12}$ =	$\frac{6}{12}$ =
$\frac{8}{16}$ =	$\frac{2}{6}$ =	$\frac{8}{12}$ =	$\frac{6}{8}$ =	$\frac{5}{10}$ =	$\frac{75}{100}$ =

Mental Math

a.	**b.**	**c.**	**d.**
e.	**f.**	**g.**	**h.**

Problem Solving

Understand

What information am I given?

What am I asked to find or do?

Plan

How can I use the information I am given?

Which strategy should I try?

Solve

Did I follow the plan?

Did I show my work?

Did I write the answer?

Check

Did I use the correct information?

Did I do what was asked?

Is my answer reasonable?

Facts	Multiply or divide as indicated.							

$\begin{array}{r} 4 \\ \times 9 \\ \hline \end{array}$	$4\overline{)16}$	$\begin{array}{r} 6 \\ \times 8 \\ \hline \end{array}$	$3\overline{)12}$	$\begin{array}{r} 5 \\ \times 7 \\ \hline \end{array}$	$4\overline{)32}$	$\begin{array}{r} 3 \\ \times 9 \\ \hline \end{array}$	$9\overline{)81}$	$\begin{array}{r} 6 \\ \times 2 \\ \hline \end{array}$	$8\overline{)64}$
$\begin{array}{r} 9 \\ \times 7 \\ \hline \end{array}$	$8\overline{)40}$	$\begin{array}{r} 2 \\ \times 4 \\ \hline \end{array}$	$6\overline{)42}$	$\begin{array}{r} 5 \\ \times 5 \\ \hline \end{array}$	$7\overline{)14}$	$\begin{array}{r} 7 \\ \times 7 \\ \hline \end{array}$	$8\overline{)8}$	$\begin{array}{r} 3 \\ \times 3 \\ \hline \end{array}$	$6\overline{)0}$
$\begin{array}{r} 7 \\ \times 3 \\ \hline \end{array}$	$2\overline{)10}$	$\begin{array}{r} 10 \\ \times 10 \\ \hline \end{array}$	$3\overline{)24}$	$\begin{array}{r} 4 \\ \times 5 \\ \hline \end{array}$	$9\overline{)54}$	$\begin{array}{r} 9 \\ \times 1 \\ \hline \end{array}$	$3\overline{)6}$	$\begin{array}{r} 7 \\ \times 4 \\ \hline \end{array}$	$7\overline{)56}$
$\begin{array}{r} 6 \\ \times 6 \\ \hline \end{array}$	$2\overline{)18}$	$\begin{array}{r} 3 \\ \times 5 \\ \hline \end{array}$	$5\overline{)30}$	$\begin{array}{r} 2 \\ \times 2 \\ \hline \end{array}$	$6\overline{)18}$	$\begin{array}{r} 9 \\ \times 5 \\ \hline \end{array}$	$6\overline{)24}$	$\begin{array}{r} 2 \\ \times 8 \\ \hline \end{array}$	$9\overline{)72}$

Mental Math			
a.	**b.**	**c.**	**d.**
e.	**f.**	**g.**	**h.**

Problem Solving

Understand
What information am I given?
What am I asked to find or do?

- -

Plan
How can I use the information I am given?
Which strategy should I try?

- -

Solve
Did I follow the plan?
Did I show my work?
Did I write the answer?

- -

Check
Did I use the correct information?
Did I do what was asked?
Is my answer reasonable?

Facts — Reduce each fraction to lowest terms.

$\frac{2}{8} =$	$\frac{4}{6} =$	$\frac{6}{10} =$	$\frac{2}{4} =$	$\frac{5}{100} =$	$\frac{9}{12} =$
$\frac{4}{10} =$	$\frac{4}{12} =$	$\frac{2}{10} =$	$\frac{3}{6} =$	$\frac{25}{100} =$	$\frac{3}{12} =$
$\frac{4}{16} =$	$\frac{3}{9} =$	$\frac{6}{9} =$	$\frac{4}{8} =$	$\frac{2}{12} =$	$\frac{6}{12} =$
$\frac{8}{16} =$	$\frac{2}{6} =$	$\frac{8}{12} =$	$\frac{6}{8} =$	$\frac{5}{10} =$	$\frac{75}{100} =$

Mental Math

a.	**b.**	**c.**	**d.**
e.	**f.**	**g.**	**h.**

Problem Solving

Understand

What information am I given?

What am I asked to find or do?

- -

Plan

How can I use the information I am given?

Which strategy should I try?

- -

Solve

Did I follow the plan?

Did I show my work?

Did I write the answer?

- -

Check

Did I use the correct information?

Did I do what was asked?

Is my answer reasonable?

Facts Multiply.

7 $\times 7$	4 $\times 6$	8 $\times 1$	2 $\times 2$	0 $\times 5$	6 $\times 3$	8 $\times 9$	5 $\times 8$	6 $\times 2$	10 $\times 10$
9 $\times 4$	2 $\times 5$	9 $\times 6$	7 $\times 3$	5 $\times 5$	7 $\times 2$	6 $\times 8$	3 $\times 5$	9 $\times 9$	5 $\times 4$
3 $\times 4$	6 $\times 5$	8 $\times 2$	4 $\times 4$	6 $\times 7$	8 $\times 8$	2 $\times 3$	7 $\times 4$	5 $\times 9$	3 $\times 8$
3 $\times 9$	7 $\times 8$	2 $\times 4$	5 $\times 7$	3 $\times 3$	9 $\times 7$	4 $\times 8$	0 $\times 0$	9 $\times 2$	6 $\times 6$

Mental Math

a.	b.	c.	d.
e.	f.	g.	h.

Problem Solving

Understand

What information am I given?

What am I asked to find or do?

- -

Plan

How can I use the information I am given?

Which strategy should I try?

- -

Solve

Did I follow the plan?

Did I show my work?

Did I write the answer?

- -

Check

Did I use the correct information?

Did I do what was asked?

Is my answer reasonable?

Facts   Reduce each fraction to lowest terms.

$\frac{2}{8}$ =	$\frac{4}{6}$ =	$\frac{6}{10}$ =	$\frac{2}{4}$ =	$\frac{5}{100}$ =	$\frac{9}{12}$ =
$\frac{4}{10}$ =	$\frac{4}{12}$ =	$\frac{2}{10}$ =	$\frac{3}{6}$ =	$\frac{25}{100}$ =	$\frac{3}{12}$ =
$\frac{4}{16}$ =	$\frac{3}{9}$ =	$\frac{6}{9}$ =	$\frac{4}{8}$ =	$\frac{2}{12}$ =	$\frac{6}{12}$ =
$\frac{8}{16}$ =	$\frac{2}{6}$ =	$\frac{8}{12}$ =	$\frac{6}{8}$ =	$\frac{5}{10}$ =	$\frac{75}{100}$ =

Mental Math

a.	**b.**	**c.**	**d.**
e.	**f.**	**g.**	**h.**

Problem Solving

Understand
What information am I given?
What am I asked to find or do?

- -

Plan
How can I use the information I am given?
Which strategy should I try?

- -

Solve
Did I follow the plan?
Did I show my work?
Did I write the answer?

- -

Check
Did I use the correct information?
Did I do what was asked?
Is my answer reasonable?

© Houghton Mifflin Harcourt Publishing Company and Stephen Hake

Facts Write each improper fraction as a mixed number. Reduce fractions.

$\frac{5}{4}$ =	$\frac{6}{4}$ =	$\frac{15}{10}$ =	$\frac{8}{3}$ =	$\frac{15}{12}$ =
$\frac{12}{8}$ =	$\frac{10}{8}$ =	$\frac{3}{2}$ =	$\frac{15}{6}$ =	$\frac{10}{4}$ =
$\frac{8}{6}$ =	$\frac{25}{10}$ =	$\frac{9}{6}$ =	$\frac{10}{6}$ =	$\frac{15}{8}$ =
$\frac{12}{10}$ =	$\frac{10}{3}$ =	$\frac{18}{12}$ =	$\frac{5}{2}$ =	$\frac{4}{3}$ =

Mental Math

a.	b.	c.	d.
e.	f.	g.	h.

Problem Solving

Understand

What information am I given?
What am I asked to find or do?

- -

Plan

How can I use the information I am given?
Which strategy should I try?

- -

Solve

Did I follow the plan?
Did I show my work?
Did I write the answer?

- -

Check

Did I use the correct information?
Did I do what was asked?
Is my answer reasonable?

Facts   Reduce each fraction to lowest terms.

$\frac{2}{8} =$	$\frac{4}{6} =$	$\frac{6}{10} =$	$\frac{2}{4} =$	$\frac{5}{100} =$	$\frac{9}{12} =$
$\frac{4}{10} =$	$\frac{4}{12} =$	$\frac{2}{10} =$	$\frac{3}{6} =$	$\frac{25}{100} =$	$\frac{3}{12} =$
$\frac{4}{16} =$	$\frac{3}{9} =$	$\frac{6}{9} =$	$\frac{4}{8} =$	$\frac{2}{12} =$	$\frac{6}{12} =$
$\frac{8}{16} =$	$\frac{2}{6} =$	$\frac{8}{12} =$	$\frac{6}{8} =$	$\frac{5}{10} =$	$\frac{75}{100} =$

Mental Math

a.	**b.**	**c.**	**d.**
e.	**f.**	**g.**	**h.**

Problem Solving

Understand
What information am I given?
What am I asked to find or do?

Plan
How can I use the information I am given?
Which strategy should I try?

Solve
Did I follow the plan?
Did I show my work?
Did I write the answer?

Check
Did I use the correct information?
Did I do what was asked?
Is my answer reasonable?

Facts   Multiply or divide as indicated.

4 × 9	4)16	6 × 8	3)12	5 × 7	4)32	3 × 9	9)81	6 × 2	8)64
9 × 7	8)40	2 × 4	6)42	5 × 5	7)14	7 × 7	8)8	3 × 3	6)0
7 × 3	2)10	10 × 10	3)24	4 × 5	9)54	9 × 1	3)6	7 × 4	7)56
6 × 6	2)18	3 × 5	5)30	2 × 2	6)18	9 × 5	6)24	2 × 8	9)72

Mental Math

a.	**b.**	**c.**	**d.**
e.	**f.**	**g.**	**h.**

Problem Solving

Understand

What information am I given?

What am I asked to find or do?

- -

Plan

How can I use the information I am given?

Which strategy should I try?

- -

Solve

Did I follow the plan?

Did I show my work?

Did I write the answer?

- -

Check

Did I use the correct information?

Did I do what was asked?

Is my answer reasonable?

| Facts | Write each improper fraction as a mixed number. Reduce fractions. |

$\frac{5}{4} =$	$\frac{6}{4} =$	$\frac{15}{10} =$	$\frac{8}{3} =$	$\frac{15}{12} =$
$\frac{12}{8} =$	$\frac{10}{8} =$	$\frac{3}{2} =$	$\frac{15}{6} =$	$\frac{10}{4} =$
$\frac{8}{6} =$	$\frac{25}{10} =$	$\frac{9}{6} =$	$\frac{10}{6} =$	$\frac{15}{8} =$
$\frac{12}{10} =$	$\frac{10}{3} =$	$\frac{18}{12} =$	$\frac{5}{2} =$	$\frac{4}{3} =$

| Mental Math |

a.	b.	c.	d.
e.	f.	g.	h.

| Problem Solving |

Understand

What information am I given?
What am I asked to find or do?

Plan

How can I use the information I am given?
Which strategy should I try?

Solve

Did I follow the plan?
Did I show my work?
Did I write the answer?

Check

Did I use the correct information?
Did I do what was asked?
Is my answer reasonable?

Facts — Reduce each fraction to lowest terms.

$\frac{2}{8}=$	$\frac{4}{6}=$	$\frac{6}{10}=$	$\frac{2}{4}=$	$\frac{5}{100}=$	$\frac{9}{12}=$
$\frac{4}{10}=$	$\frac{4}{12}=$	$\frac{2}{10}=$	$\frac{3}{6}=$	$\frac{25}{100}=$	$\frac{3}{12}=$
$\frac{4}{16}=$	$\frac{3}{9}=$	$\frac{6}{9}=$	$\frac{4}{8}=$	$\frac{2}{12}=$	$\frac{6}{12}=$
$\frac{8}{16}=$	$\frac{2}{6}=$	$\frac{8}{12}=$	$\frac{6}{8}=$	$\frac{5}{10}=$	$\frac{75}{100}=$

Mental Math

a.	b.	c.	d.
e.	f.	g.	h.

Problem Solving

Understand

What information am I given?

What am I asked to find or do?

Plan

How can I use the information I am given?

Which strategy should I try?

Solve

Did I follow the plan?

Did I show my work?

Did I write the answer?

Check

Did I use the correct information?

Did I do what was asked?

Is my answer reasonable?

| **Facts** | Write each improper fraction as a mixed number. Reduce fractions. |

$\frac{5}{4} =$	$\frac{6}{4} =$	$\frac{15}{10} =$	$\frac{8}{3} =$	$\frac{15}{12} =$
$\frac{12}{8} =$	$\frac{10}{8} =$	$\frac{3}{2} =$	$\frac{15}{6} =$	$\frac{10}{4} =$
$\frac{8}{6} =$	$\frac{25}{10} =$	$\frac{9}{6} =$	$\frac{10}{6} =$	$\frac{15}{8} =$
$\frac{12}{10} =$	$\frac{10}{3} =$	$\frac{18}{12} =$	$\frac{5}{2} =$	$\frac{4}{3} =$

Mental Math

a.	b.	c.	d.
e.	f.	g.	h.

Problem Solving

Understand

What information am I given?

What am I asked to find or do?

- -

Plan

How can I use the information I am given?

Which strategy should I try?

- -

Solve

Did I follow the plan?

Did I show my work?

Did I write the answer?

- -

Check

Did I use the correct information?

Did I do what was asked?

Is my answer reasonable?

Facts		Multiply or divide as indicated.							
4 × 9	4)̅1̅6̅	6 × 8	3)̅1̅2̅	5 × 7	4)̅3̅2̅	3 × 9	9)̅8̅1̅	6 × 2	8)̅6̅4̅
9 × 7	8)̅4̅0̅	2 × 4	6)̅4̅2̅	5 × 5	7)̅1̅4̅	7 × 7	8)̅8̅	3 × 3	6)̅0̅
7 × 3	2)̅1̅0̅	10 × 10	3)̅2̅4̅	4 × 5	9)̅5̅4̅	9 × 1	3)̅6̅	7 × 4	7)̅5̅6̅
6 × 6	2)̅1̅8̅	3 × 5	5)̅3̅0̅	2 × 2	6)̅1̅8̅	9 × 5	6)̅2̅4̅	2 × 8	9)̅7̅2̅

Mental Math

a.	b.	c.	d.
e.	f.	g.	h.

Problem Solving

Understand
What information am I given?
What am I asked to find or do?

Plan
How can I use the information I am given?
Which strategy should I try?

Solve
Did I follow the plan?
Did I show my work?
Did I write the answer?

Check
Did I use the correct information?
Did I do what was asked?
Is my answer reasonable?

Facts   Reduce each fraction to lowest terms.

$\frac{2}{8}$ =	$\frac{4}{6}$ =	$\frac{6}{10}$ =	$\frac{2}{4}$ =	$\frac{5}{100}$ =	$\frac{9}{12}$ =
$\frac{4}{10}$ =	$\frac{4}{12}$ =	$\frac{2}{10}$ =	$\frac{3}{6}$ =	$\frac{25}{100}$ =	$\frac{3}{12}$ =
$\frac{4}{16}$ =	$\frac{3}{9}$ =	$\frac{6}{9}$ =	$\frac{4}{8}$ =	$\frac{2}{12}$ =	$\frac{6}{12}$ =
$\frac{8}{16}$ =	$\frac{2}{6}$ =	$\frac{8}{12}$ =	$\frac{6}{8}$ =	$\frac{5}{10}$ =	$\frac{75}{100}$ =

Mental Math

a.	b.	c.	d.
e.	f.	g.	h.

Problem Solving

Understand

What information am I given?

What am I asked to find or do?

Plan

How can I use the information I am given?

Which strategy should I try?

Solve

Did I follow the plan?

Did I show my work?

Did I write the answer?

Check

Did I use the correct information?

Did I do what was asked?

Is my answer reasonable?

Name _____ Time _____

Facts   Multiply.

7 × 7	4 × 6	8 × 1	2 × 2	0 × 5	6 × 3	8 × 9	5 × 8	6 × 2	10 × 10
9 × 4	2 × 5	9 × 6	7 × 3	5 × 5	7 × 2	6 × 8	3 × 5	9 × 9	5 × 4
3 × 4	6 × 5	8 × 2	4 × 4	6 × 7	8 × 8	2 × 3	7 × 4	5 × 9	3 × 8
3 × 9	7 × 8	2 × 4	5 × 7	3 × 3	9 × 7	4 × 8	0 × 0	9 × 2	6 × 6

Mental Math

a.	b.	c.	d.
e.	f.	g.	h.

Problem Solving

Understand

What information am I given?
What am I asked to find or do?

Plan

How can I use the information I am given?
Which strategy should I try?

Solve

Did I follow the plan?
Did I show my work?
Did I write the answer?

Check

Did I use the correct information?
Did I do what was asked?
Is my answer reasonable?

Facts   Write each mixed number as an improper fraction.

$2\frac{1}{2} =$	$2\frac{2}{5} =$	$1\frac{3}{4} =$	$2\frac{3}{4} =$	$2\frac{1}{8} =$
$1\frac{2}{3} =$	$3\frac{1}{2} =$	$1\frac{5}{6} =$	$2\frac{1}{4} =$	$1\frac{1}{8} =$
$5\frac{1}{2} =$	$1\frac{3}{8} =$	$5\frac{1}{3} =$	$3\frac{1}{4} =$	$4\frac{1}{2} =$
$1\frac{7}{8} =$	$2\frac{2}{3} =$	$1\frac{5}{8} =$	$3\frac{3}{4} =$	$7\frac{1}{2} =$

Mental Math

a.	b.	c.	d.
e.	f.	g.	h.

Problem Solving

Understand
What information am I given?
What am I asked to find or do?

- -

Plan
How can I use the information I am given?
Which strategy should I try?

- -

Solve
Did I follow the plan?
Did I show my work?
Did I write the answer?

- -

Check
Did I use the correct information?
Did I do what was asked?
Is my answer reasonable?

| Facts | | Multiply or divide as indicated. | | | | | |

4 × 9	4)16	6 × 8	3)12	5 × 7	4)32	3 × 9	9)81	6 × 2	8)64
9 × 7	8)40	2 × 4	6)42	5 × 5	7)14	7 × 7	8)8	3 × 3	6)0
7 × 3	2)10	10 × 10	3)24	4 × 5	9)54	9 × 1	3)6	7 × 4	7)56
6 × 6	2)18	3 × 5	5)30	2 × 2	6)18	9 × 5	6)24	2 × 8	9)72

Mental Math

a.	b.	c.	d.
e.	f.	g.	h.

Problem Solving

Understand

What information am I given?

What am I asked to find or do?

Plan

How can I use the information I am given?

Which strategy should I try?

Solve

Did I follow the plan?

Did I show my work?

Did I write the answer?

Check

Did I use the correct information?

Did I do what was asked?

Is my answer reasonable?

Facts   Write each mixed number as an improper fraction.

$2\frac{1}{2} =$	$2\frac{2}{5} =$	$1\frac{3}{4} =$	$2\frac{3}{4} =$	$2\frac{1}{8} =$
$1\frac{2}{3} =$	$3\frac{1}{2} =$	$1\frac{5}{6} =$	$2\frac{1}{4} =$	$1\frac{1}{8} =$
$5\frac{1}{2} =$	$1\frac{3}{8} =$	$5\frac{1}{3} =$	$3\frac{1}{4} =$	$4\frac{1}{2} =$
$1\frac{7}{8} =$	$2\frac{2}{3} =$	$1\frac{5}{8} =$	$3\frac{3}{4} =$	$7\frac{1}{2} =$

Mental Math

a.	**b.**	**c.**	**d.**
e.	**f.**	**g.**	**h.**

Problem Solving

Understand
What information am I given?
What am I asked to find or do?

Plan
How can I use the information I am given?
Which strategy should I try?

Solve
Did I follow the plan?
Did I show my work?
Did I write the answer?

Check
Did I use the correct information?
Did I do what was asked?
Is my answer reasonable?

Facts Write each mixed number as an improper fraction.

$2\frac{1}{2} =$	$2\frac{2}{5} =$	$1\frac{3}{4} =$	$2\frac{3}{4} =$	$2\frac{1}{8} =$
$1\frac{2}{3} =$	$3\frac{1}{2} =$	$1\frac{5}{6} =$	$2\frac{1}{4} =$	$1\frac{1}{8} =$
$5\frac{1}{2} =$	$1\frac{3}{8} =$	$5\frac{1}{3} =$	$3\frac{1}{4} =$	$4\frac{1}{2} =$
$1\frac{7}{8} =$	$2\frac{2}{3} =$	$1\frac{5}{8} =$	$3\frac{3}{4} =$	$7\frac{1}{2} =$

Mental Math

a.	**b.**	**c.**	**d.**
e.	**f.**	**g.**	**h.**

Problem Solving

Understand
What information am I given?
What am I asked to find or do?

- -

Plan
How can I use the information I am given?
Which strategy should I try?

- -

Solve
Did I follow the plan?
Did I show my work?
Did I write the answer?

- -

Check
Did I use the correct information?
Did I do what was asked?
Is my answer reasonable?

Facts   Write each improper fraction as a mixed number. Reduce fractions.

$\frac{5}{4}=$	$\frac{6}{4}=$	$\frac{15}{10}=$	$\frac{8}{3}=$	$\frac{15}{12}=$
$\frac{12}{8}=$	$\frac{10}{8}=$	$\frac{3}{2}=$	$\frac{15}{6}=$	$\frac{10}{4}=$
$\frac{8}{6}=$	$\frac{25}{10}=$	$\frac{9}{6}=$	$\frac{10}{6}=$	$\frac{15}{8}=$
$\frac{12}{10}=$	$\frac{10}{3}=$	$\frac{18}{12}=$	$\frac{5}{2}=$	$\frac{4}{3}=$

Mental Math

a.	**b.**	**c.**	**d.**
e.	**f.**	**g.**	**h.**

Problem Solving

Understand

What information am I given?

What am I asked to find or do?

- -

Plan

How can I use the information I am given?

Which strategy should I try?

- -

Solve

Did I follow the plan?

Did I show my work?

Did I write the answer?

- -

Check

Did I use the correct information?

Did I do what was asked?

Is my answer reasonable?

Saxon Math Course 1

Facts   Write each mixed number as an improper fraction.

$2\frac{1}{2} =$	$2\frac{2}{5} =$	$1\frac{3}{4} =$	$2\frac{3}{4} =$	$2\frac{1}{8} =$
$1\frac{2}{3} =$	$3\frac{1}{2} =$	$1\frac{5}{6} =$	$2\frac{1}{4} =$	$1\frac{1}{8} =$
$5\frac{1}{2} =$	$1\frac{3}{8} =$	$5\frac{1}{3} =$	$3\frac{1}{4} =$	$4\frac{1}{2} =$
$1\frac{7}{8} =$	$2\frac{2}{3} =$	$1\frac{5}{8} =$	$3\frac{3}{4} =$	$7\frac{1}{2} =$

Mental Math

a.	b.	c.	d.
e.	f.	g.	h.

Problem Solving

Understand
What information am I given?
What am I asked to find or do?

- -

Plan
How can I use the information I am given?
Which strategy should I try?

- -

Solve
Did I follow the plan?
Did I show my work?
Did I write the answer?

- -

Check
Did I use the correct information?
Did I do what was asked?
Is my answer reasonable?

Facts   Reduce each fraction to lowest terms.

$\frac{2}{8}$ =	$\frac{4}{6}$ =	$\frac{6}{10}$ =	$\frac{2}{4}$ =	$\frac{5}{100}$ =	$\frac{9}{12}$ =
$\frac{4}{10}$ =	$\frac{4}{12}$ =	$\frac{2}{10}$ =	$\frac{3}{6}$ =	$\frac{25}{100}$ =	$\frac{3}{12}$ =
$\frac{4}{16}$ =	$\frac{3}{9}$ =	$\frac{6}{9}$ =	$\frac{4}{8}$ =	$\frac{2}{12}$ =	$\frac{6}{12}$ =
$\frac{8}{16}$ =	$\frac{2}{6}$ =	$\frac{8}{12}$ =	$\frac{6}{8}$ =	$\frac{5}{10}$ =	$\frac{75}{100}$ =

Mental Math

a.	**b.**	**c.**	**d.**
e.	**f.**	**g.**	**h.**

Problem Solving

Understand

What information am I given?

What am I asked to find or do?

- -

Plan

How can I use the information I am given?

Which strategy should I try?

- -

Solve

Did I follow the plan?

Did I show my work?

Did I write the answer?

- -

Check

Did I use the correct information?

Did I do what was asked?

Is my answer reasonable?

Facts   Multiply.

7 ×7	4 ×6	8 ×1	2 ×2	0 ×5	6 ×3	8 ×9	5 ×8	6 ×2	10 ×10
9 ×4	2 ×5	9 ×6	7 ×3	5 ×5	7 ×2	6 ×8	3 ×5	9 ×9	5 ×4
3 ×4	6 ×5	8 ×2	4 ×4	6 ×7	8 ×8	2 ×3	7 ×4	5 ×9	3 ×8
3 ×9	7 ×8	2 ×4	5 ×7	3 ×3	9 ×7	4 ×8	0 ×0	9 ×2	6 ×6

Mental Math

a.	b.	c.	d.
e.	**f.**	**g.**	**h.**

Problem Solving

Understand

What information am I given?

What am I asked to find or do?

Plan

How can I use the information I am given?

Which strategy should I try?

Solve

Did I follow the plan?

Did I show my work?

Did I write the answer?

Check

Did I use the correct information?

Did I do what was asked?

Is my answer reasonable?

Facts Multiply or divide as indicated.

4 × 9	4)‾16	6 × 8	3)‾12	5 × 7	4)‾32	3 × 9	9)‾81	6 × 2	8)‾64
9 × 7	8)‾40	2 × 4	6)‾42	5 × 5	7)‾14	7 × 7	8)‾8	3 × 3	6)‾0
7 × 3	2)‾10	10 × 10	3)‾24	4 × 5	9)‾54	9 × 1	3)‾6	7 × 4	7)‾56
6 × 6	2)‾18	3 × 5	5)‾30	2 × 2	6)‾18	9 × 5	6)‾24	2 × 8	9)‾72

Mental Math

a.	**b.**	**c.**	**d.**
e.	**f.**	**g.**	**h.**

Problem Solving

Understand

What information am I given?

What am I asked to find or do?

- -

Plan

How can I use the information I am given?

Which strategy should I try?

- -

Solve

Did I follow the plan?

Did I show my work?

Did I write the answer?

- -

Check

Did I use the correct information?

Did I do what was asked?

Is my answer reasonable?

© Houghton Mifflin Harcourt Publishing Company and Stephen Hake

Facts — Write each mixed number as an improper fraction.

$2\frac{1}{2} =$	$2\frac{2}{5} =$	$1\frac{3}{4} =$	$2\frac{3}{4} =$	$2\frac{1}{8} =$
$1\frac{2}{3} =$	$3\frac{1}{2} =$	$1\frac{5}{6} =$	$2\frac{1}{4} =$	$1\frac{1}{8} =$
$5\frac{1}{2} =$	$1\frac{3}{8} =$	$5\frac{1}{3} =$	$3\frac{1}{4} =$	$4\frac{1}{2} =$
$1\frac{7}{8} =$	$2\frac{2}{3} =$	$1\frac{5}{8} =$	$3\frac{3}{4} =$	$7\frac{1}{2} =$

Mental Math

a.	**b.**	**c.**	**d.**
e.	**f.**	**g.**	**h.**

Problem Solving

Understand

What information am I given?

What am I asked to find or do?

Plan

How can I use the information I am given?

Which strategy should I try?

Solve

Did I follow the plan?

Did I show my work?

Did I write the answer?

Check

Did I use the correct information?

Did I do what was asked?

Is my answer reasonable?

Facts   Write each improper fraction as a mixed number. Reduce fractions.

$\frac{5}{4} =$	$\frac{6}{4} =$	$\frac{15}{10} =$	$\frac{8}{3} =$	$\frac{15}{12} =$
$\frac{12}{8} =$	$\frac{10}{8} =$	$\frac{3}{2} =$	$\frac{15}{6} =$	$\frac{10}{4} =$
$\frac{8}{6} =$	$\frac{25}{10} =$	$\frac{9}{6} =$	$\frac{10}{6} =$	$\frac{15}{8} =$
$\frac{12}{10} =$	$\frac{10}{3} =$	$\frac{18}{12} =$	$\frac{5}{2} =$	$\frac{4}{3} =$

Mental Math

a.	**b.**	**c.**	**d.**
e.	**f.**	**g.**	**h.**

Problem Solving

Understand

What information am I given?

What am I asked to find or do?

- -

Plan

How can I use the information I am given?

Which strategy should I try?

- -

Solve

Did I follow the plan?

Did I show my work?

Did I write the answer?

- -

Check

Did I use the correct information?

Did I do what was asked?

Is my answer reasonable?

Facts

Complete each equivalent measure.		Write a unit for each reference.

Metric Units:

1. 1 cm = _____ mm	13. 10 cm = _____ mm	25. The thickness of a dime:
2. 1 m = _____ mm	14. 2 m = _____ cm	_____
3. 1 m = _____ cm	15. 5 km = _____ m	26. The width of a little finger:
4. 1 km = _____ m	16. 2.5 cm = _____ mm	_____
5. 1 in. = _____ cm	17. 1.5 m = _____ cm	27. The length of one big step:
6. 1 mi ≈ _____ m	18. 7.5 km = _____ m	_____

U.S. Customary Units:

7. 1 ft = _____ in.	19. $\frac{1}{2}$ ft = _____ in.	28. The width of two fingers:
8. 1 yd = _____ in.	20. 2 ft = _____ in.	_____
9. 1 yd = _____ ft	21. 3 ft = _____ in.	29. The length of a man's shoe:
10. 1 mi = _____ ft	22. 2 yd = _____ ft	_____
11. 1 m ≈ _____ in.	23. 10 yd = _____ ft	30. The length of one big step:
12. 1 km ≈ _____ mi	24. 100 yd = _____ ft	_____

Mental Math

a.	b.	c.	d.
e.	f.	g.	h.

Problem Solving

Understand

What information am I given?

What am I asked to find or do?

Plan

How can I use the information I am given?

Which strategy should I try?

Solve

Did I follow the plan?

Did I show my work?

Did I write the answer?

Check

Did I use the correct information?

Did I do what was asked?

Is my answer reasonable?

Facts   Reduce each fraction to lowest terms.

$\dfrac{2}{8}=$	$\dfrac{4}{6}=$	$\dfrac{6}{10}=$	$\dfrac{2}{4}=$	$\dfrac{5}{100}=$	$\dfrac{9}{12}=$
$\dfrac{4}{10}=$	$\dfrac{4}{12}=$	$\dfrac{2}{10}=$	$\dfrac{3}{6}=$	$\dfrac{25}{100}=$	$\dfrac{3}{12}=$
$\dfrac{4}{16}=$	$\dfrac{3}{9}=$	$\dfrac{6}{9}=$	$\dfrac{4}{8}=$	$\dfrac{2}{12}=$	$\dfrac{6}{12}=$
$\dfrac{8}{16}=$	$\dfrac{2}{6}=$	$\dfrac{8}{12}=$	$\dfrac{6}{8}=$	$\dfrac{5}{10}=$	$\dfrac{75}{100}=$

Mental Math

a.	**b.**	**c.**	**d.**
e.	**f.**	**g.**	**h.**

Problem Solving

Understand

What information am I given?

What am I asked to find or do?

Plan

How can I use the information I am given?

Which strategy should I try?

Solve

Did I follow the plan?

Did I show my work?

Did I write the answer?

Check

Did I use the correct information?

Did I do what was asked?

Is my answer reasonable?

Facts

Complete each equivalent measure.		Write a unit for each reference.

Complete each equivalent measure.

1. 1 cm = _____ mm
2. 1 m = _____ mm
3. 1 m = _____ cm
4. 1 km = _____ m

5. 1 in. = _____ cm
6. 1 mi ≈ _____ m

7. 1 ft = _____ in.
8. 1 yd = _____ in.
9. 1 yd = _____ ft
10. 1 mi = _____ ft

11. 1 m ≈ _____ in.
12. 1 km ≈ _____ mi

13. 10 cm = _____ mm
14. 2 m = _____ cm
15. 5 km = _____ m
16. 2.5 cm = _____ mm
17. 1.5 m = _____ cm
18. 7.5 km = _____ m

19. $\frac{1}{2}$ ft = _____ in.
20. 2 ft = _____ in.
21. 3 ft = _____ in.
22. 2 yd = _____ ft
23. 10 yd = _____ ft
24. 100 yd = _____ ft

Write a unit for each reference.

Metric Units:
25. The thickness of a dime:
   _____
26. The width of a little finger:
   _____
27. The length of one big step:
   _____

U.S. Customary Units:
28. The width of two fingers:
   _____
29. The length of a man's shoe:
   _____
30. The length of one big step:
   _____

Mental Math

a.	b.	c.	d.
e.	f.	g.	h.

Problem Solving

Understand

What information am I given?
What am I asked to find or do?

Plan

How can I use the information I am given?
Which strategy should I try?

Solve

Did I follow the plan?
Did I show my work?
Did I write the answer?

Check

Did I use the correct information?
Did I do what was asked?
Is my answer reasonable?

Facts   Write each mixed number as an improper fraction.

$2\frac{1}{2}$ =	$2\frac{2}{5}$ =	$1\frac{3}{4}$ =	$2\frac{3}{4}$ =	$2\frac{1}{8}$ =
$1\frac{2}{3}$ =	$3\frac{1}{2}$ =	$1\frac{5}{6}$ =	$2\frac{1}{4}$ =	$1\frac{1}{8}$ =
$5\frac{1}{2}$ =	$1\frac{3}{8}$ =	$5\frac{1}{3}$ =	$3\frac{1}{4}$ =	$4\frac{1}{2}$ =
$1\frac{7}{8}$ =	$2\frac{2}{3}$ =	$1\frac{5}{8}$ =	$3\frac{3}{4}$ =	$7\frac{1}{2}$ =

Mental Math

a.	**b.**	**c.**	**d.**
e.	**f.**	**g.**	**h.**

Problem Solving

Understand

What information am I given?

What am I asked to find or do?

- -

Plan

How can I use the information I am given?

Which strategy should I try?

- -

Solve

Did I follow the plan?

Did I show my work?

Did I write the answer?

- -

Check

Did I use the correct information?

Did I do what was asked?

Is my answer reasonable?

Facts

Complete each equivalent measure.		Write a unit for each reference.
1. 1 cm = _____ mm	13. 10 cm = _____ mm	**Metric Units:**
2. 1 m = _____ mm	14. 2 m = _____ cm	25. The thickness of a dime:
3. 1 m = _____ cm	15. 5 km = _____ m	_____
4. 1 km = _____ m	16. 2.5 cm = _____ mm	26. The width of a little finger:
5. 1 in. = _____ cm	17. 1.5 m = _____ cm	_____
6. 1 mi ≈ _____ m	18. 7.5 km = _____ m	27. The length of one big step:
		_____
7. 1 ft = _____ in.	19. $\frac{1}{2}$ ft = _____ in.	**U.S. Customary Units:**
8. 1 yd = _____ in.	20. 2 ft = _____ in.	28. The width of two fingers:
9. 1 yd = _____ ft	21. 3 ft = _____ in.	_____
10. 1 mi = _____ ft	22. 2 yd = _____ ft	29. The length of a man's shoe:
11. 1 m ≈ _____ in.	23. 10 yd = _____ ft	_____
12. 1 km ≈ _____ mi	24. 100 yd = _____ ft	30. The length of one big step:
		_____

Mental Math

a.	b.	c.	d.
e.	f.	g.	h.

Problem Solving

Understand

What information am I given?

What am I asked to find or do?

- -

Plan

How can I use the information I am given?

Which strategy should I try?

- -

Solve

Did I follow the plan?

Did I show my work?

Did I write the answer?

- -

Check

Did I use the correct information?

Did I do what was asked?

Is my answer reasonable?

| Facts | Write each improper fraction as a mixed number. Reduce fractions. |

$\frac{5}{4} =$	$\frac{6}{4} =$	$\frac{15}{10} =$	$\frac{8}{3} =$	$\frac{15}{12} =$
$\frac{12}{8} =$	$\frac{10}{8} =$	$\frac{3}{2} =$	$\frac{15}{6} =$	$\frac{10}{4} =$
$\frac{8}{6} =$	$\frac{25}{10} =$	$\frac{9}{6} =$	$\frac{10}{6} =$	$\frac{15}{8} =$
$\frac{12}{10} =$	$\frac{10}{3} =$	$\frac{18}{12} =$	$\frac{5}{2} =$	$\frac{4}{3} =$

Mental Math

a.	b.	c.	d.
e.	f.	g.	h.

Problem Solving

Understand

What information am I given?

What am I asked to find or do?

Plan

How can I use the information I am given?

Which strategy should I try?

Solve

Did I follow the plan?

Did I show my work?

Did I write the answer?

Check

Did I use the correct information?

Did I do what was asked?

Is my answer reasonable?

Facts

Complete each equivalent measure.		Write a unit for each reference.

Complete each equivalent measure.

1. 1 cm = _____ mm
2. 1 m = _____ mm
3. 1 m = _____ cm
4. 1 km = _____ m

5. 1 in. = _____ cm
6. 1 mi ≈ _____ m

7. 1 ft = _____ in.
8. 1 yd = _____ in.
9. 1 yd = _____ ft
10. 1 mi = _____ ft

11. 1 m ≈ _____ in.
12. 1 km ≈ _____ mi

13. 10 cm = _____ mm
14. 2 m = _____ cm
15. 5 km = _____ m
16. 2.5 cm = _____ mm
17. 1.5 m = _____ cm
18. 7.5 km = _____ m

19. $\frac{1}{2}$ ft = _____ in.
20. 2 ft = _____ in.
21. 3 ft = _____ in.
22. 2 yd = _____ ft
23. 10 yd = _____ ft
24. 100 yd = _____ ft

Write a unit for each reference.

Metric Units:

25. The thickness of a dime:
_____

26. The width of a little finger:
_____

27. The length of one big step:
_____

U.S. Customary Units:

28. The width of two fingers:
_____

29. The length of a man's shoe:
_____

30. The length of one big step:
_____

Mental Math

a.	b.	c.	d.
e.	f.	g.	h.

Problem Solving

Understand

What information am I given?
What am I asked to find or do?

- -

Plan

How can I use the information I am given?
Which strategy should I try?

- -

Solve

Did I follow the plan?
Did I show my work?
Did I write the answer?

- -

Check

Did I use the correct information?
Did I do what was asked?
Is my answer reasonable?

Facts

Write the abbreviation.	Complete each equivalence.	Complete each conversion.
Metric Units:	Metric Units:	14. 2 liters = _____ milliliters
1. liter _____	7. 1 liter = _____ milliliters	15. 2 liters ≈ _____ quarts
2. milliliter _____	U.S. Customary Units:	16. 3.78 liters = _____ milliliters
U.S. Customary Units:	8. 1 cup = _____ ounces	17. 0.5 liter = _____ milliliters
3. ounces _____	9. 1 pint = _____ ounces	18. $\frac{1}{2}$ gallon = _____ quarts
4. pint _____	10. 1 pint = _____ cups	19. 2 gallons = _____ quarts
5. quart _____	11. 1 quart = _____ pints	20. 2 half gallons = _____ gallon
6. gallon _____	12. 1 gallon = _____ quarts	21. 8 cups = _____ quarts
	Between Systems:	22–23. A two-liter bottle is a little more than _____ quarts or _____ gallon.
	13. 1 liter ≈ _____ quart	

Mental Math

a.	b.	c.	d.
e.	f.	g.	h.

Problem Solving

Understand
What information am I given?
What am I asked to find or do?

- -

Plan
How can I use the information I am given?
Which strategy should I try?

- -

Solve
Did I follow the plan?
Did I show my work?
Did I write the answer?

- -

Check
Did I use the correct information?
Did I do what was asked?
Is my answer reasonable?

Facts	Write each improper fraction as a mixed number. Reduce fractions.			
$\frac{5}{4} =$	$\frac{6}{4} =$	$\frac{15}{10} =$	$\frac{8}{3} =$	$\frac{15}{12} =$
$\frac{12}{8} =$	$\frac{10}{8} =$	$\frac{3}{2} =$	$\frac{15}{6} =$	$\frac{10}{4} =$
$\frac{8}{6} =$	$\frac{25}{10} =$	$\frac{9}{6} =$	$\frac{10}{6} =$	$\frac{15}{8} =$
$\frac{12}{10} =$	$\frac{10}{3} =$	$\frac{18}{12} =$	$\frac{5}{2} =$	$\frac{4}{3} =$

Mental Math

a.	b.	c.	d.
e.	f.	g.	h.

Problem Solving

Understand

What information am I given?

What am I asked to find or do?

- -

Plan

How can I use the information I am given?

Which strategy should I try?

- -

Solve

Did I follow the plan?

Did I show my work?

Did I write the answer?

- -

Check

Did I use the correct information?

Did I do what was asked?

Is my answer reasonable?

Facts

Complete each equivalent measure.		Write a unit for each reference.
1. 1 cm = _____ mm	13. 10 cm = _____ mm	**Metric Units:**
2. 1 m = _____ mm	14. 2 m = _____ cm	25. The thickness of a dime:
3. 1 m = _____ cm	15. 5 km = _____ m	_____
4. 1 km = _____ m	16. 2.5 cm = _____ mm	26. The width of a little finger:
5. 1 in. = _____ cm	17. 1.5 m = _____ cm	_____
6. 1 mi ≈ _____ m	18. 7.5 km = _____ m	27. The length of one big step:
		_____
7. 1 ft = _____ in.	19. $\frac{1}{2}$ ft = _____ in.	**U.S. Customary Units:**
8. 1 yd = _____ in.	20. 2 ft = _____ in.	28. The width of two fingers:
9. 1 yd = _____ ft	21. 3 ft = _____ in.	_____
10. 1 mi = _____ ft	22. 2 yd = _____ ft	29. The length of a man's shoe:
11. 1 m ≈ _____ in.	23. 10 yd = _____ ft	_____
12. 1 km ≈ _____ mi	24. 100 yd = _____ ft	30. The length of one big step:
		_____

Mental Math

a.	b.	c.	d.
e.	f.	g.	h.

Problem Solving

Understand

What information am I given?
What am I asked to find or do?

Plan

How can I use the information I am given?
Which strategy should I try?

Solve

Did I follow the plan?
Did I show my work?
Did I write the answer?

Check

Did I use the correct information?
Did I do what was asked?
Is my answer reasonable?

Facts

Write the abbreviation.	Complete each equivalence.	Complete each conversion.
Metric Units:	Metric Units:	14. 2 liters = _____ milliliters
1. liter _____	7. 1 liter = _____ milliliters	15. 2 liters ≈ _____ quarts
2. milliliter _____	U.S. Customary Units:	16. 3.78 liters = _____ milliliters
U.S. Customary Units:	8. 1 cup = _____ ounces	17. 0.5 liter = _____ milliliters
3. ounces _____	9. 1 pint = _____ ounces	18. $\frac{1}{2}$ gallon = _____ quarts
4. pint _____	10. 1 pint = _____ cups	19. 2 gallons = _____ quarts
5. quart _____	11. 1 quart = _____ pints	20. 2 half gallons = _____ gallon
6. gallon _____	12. 1 gallon = _____ quarts	21. 8 cups = _____ quarts
	Between Systems:	22–23. A two-liter bottle is a little more than _____ quarts or _____ gallon.
	13. 1 liter ≈ _____ quart	

Mental Math

a.	b.	c.	d.
e.	f.	g.	h.

Problem Solving

Understand
What information am I given?
What am I asked to find or do?

Plan
How can I use the information I am given?
Which strategy should I try?

Solve
Did I follow the plan?
Did I show my work?
Did I write the answer?

Check
Did I use the correct information?
Did I do what was asked?
Is my answer reasonable?

Facts   Reduce each fraction to lowest terms.

$\frac{2}{8} =$	$\frac{4}{6} =$	$\frac{6}{10} =$	$\frac{2}{4} =$	$\frac{5}{100} =$	$\frac{9}{12} =$
$\frac{4}{10} =$	$\frac{4}{12} =$	$\frac{2}{10} =$	$\frac{3}{6} =$	$\frac{25}{100} =$	$\frac{3}{12} =$
$\frac{4}{16} =$	$\frac{3}{9} =$	$\frac{6}{9} =$	$\frac{4}{8} =$	$\frac{2}{12} =$	$\frac{6}{12} =$
$\frac{8}{16} =$	$\frac{2}{6} =$	$\frac{8}{12} =$	$\frac{6}{8} =$	$\frac{5}{10} =$	$\frac{75}{100} =$

Mental Math

a.	b.	c.	d.
e.	f.	g.	h.

Problem Solving

Understand

What information am I given?

What am I asked to find or do?

Plan

How can I use the information I am given?

Which strategy should I try?

Solve

Did I follow the plan?

Did I show my work?

Did I write the answer?

Check

Did I use the correct information?

Did I do what was asked?

Is my answer reasonable?

Facts   Multiply.

7 × 7	4 × 6	8 × 1	2 × 2	0 × 5	6 × 3	8 × 9	5 × 8	6 × 2	10 × 10
9 × 4	2 × 5	9 × 6	7 × 3	5 × 5	7 × 2	6 × 8	3 × 5	9 × 9	5 × 4
3 × 4	6 × 5	8 × 2	4 × 4	6 × 7	8 × 8	2 × 3	7 × 4	5 × 9	3 × 8
3 × 9	7 × 8	2 × 4	5 × 7	3 × 3	9 × 7	4 × 8	0 × 0	9 × 2	6 × 6

Mental Math

a.	b.	c.	d.
e.	f.	g.	h.

Problem Solving

Understand

What information am I given?
What am I asked to find or do?

- -

Plan

How can I use the information I am given?
Which strategy should I try?

- -

Solve

Did I follow the plan?
Did I show my work?
Did I write the answer?

- -

Check

Did I use the correct information?
Did I do what was asked?
Is my answer reasonable?

Name _____ Time _____

Facts

Write the abbreviation.	Complete each equivalence.	Complete each conversion.
Metric Units:	Metric Units:	14. 2 liters = _____ milliliters
1. liter _____	7. 1 liter = _____ milliliters	15. 2 liters ≈ _____ quarts
2. milliliter _____	U.S. Customary Units:	16. 3.78 liters = _____ milliliters
U.S. Customary Units:	8. 1 cup = _____ ounces	17. 0.5 liter = _____ milliliters
3. ounces _____	9. 1 pint = _____ ounces	18. $\frac{1}{2}$ gallon = _____ quarts
4. pint _____	10. 1 pint = _____ cups	19. 2 gallons = _____ quarts
5. quart _____	11. 1 quart = _____ pints	20. 2 half gallons = _____ gallon
6. gallon _____	12. 1 gallon = _____ quarts	21. 8 cups = _____ quarts
	Between Systems:	22–23. A two-liter bottle is a little more than _____ quarts or _____ gallon.
	13. 1 liter ≈ _____ quart	

Mental Math

a.	b.	c.	d.
e.	f.	g.	h.

Problem Solving

Understand

What information am I given?
What am I asked to find or do?

Plan

How can I use the information I am given?
Which strategy should I try?

Solve

Did I follow the plan?
Did I show my work?
Did I write the answer?

Check

Did I use the correct information?
Did I do what was asked?
Is my answer reasonable?

Facts

Complete each equivalent measure.		Write a unit for each reference.

Complete each equivalent measure.

1. 1 cm = _____ mm
2. 1 m = _____ mm
3. 1 m = _____ cm
4. 1 km = _____ m
5. 1 in. = _____ cm
6. 1 mi ≈ _____ m

7. 1 ft = _____ in.
8. 1 yd = _____ in.
9. 1 yd = _____ ft
10. 1 mi = _____ ft
11. 1 m ≈ _____ in.
12. 1 km ≈ _____ mi

13. 10 cm = _____ mm
14. 2 m = _____ cm
15. 5 km = _____ m
16. 2.5 cm = _____ mm
17. 1.5 m = _____ cm
18. 7.5 km = _____ m

19. $\frac{1}{2}$ ft = _____ in.
20. 2 ft = _____ in.
21. 3 ft = _____ in.
22. 2 yd = _____ ft
23. 10 yd = _____ ft
24. 100 yd = _____ ft

Write a unit for each reference.

Metric Units:

25. The thickness of a dime:
_____

26. The width of a little finger:
_____

27. The length of one big step:
_____

U.S. Customary Units:

28. The width of two fingers:
_____

29. The length of a man's shoe:
_____

30. The length of one big step:
_____

Mental Math

a.	b.	c.	d.
e.	f.	g.	h.

Problem Solving

Understand
What information am I given?
What am I asked to find or do?

Plan
How can I use the information I am given?
Which strategy should I try?

Solve
Did I follow the plan?
Did I show my work?
Did I write the answer?

Check
Did I use the correct information?
Did I do what was asked?
Is my answer reasonable?

Power Up | **J**

Use with **Lesson 90**

| Facts | Write each mixed number as an improper fraction. |

$2\frac{1}{2} =$	$2\frac{2}{5} =$	$1\frac{3}{4} =$	$2\frac{3}{4} =$	$2\frac{1}{8} =$
$1\frac{2}{3} =$	$3\frac{1}{2} =$	$1\frac{5}{6} =$	$2\frac{1}{4} =$	$1\frac{1}{8} =$
$5\frac{1}{2} =$	$1\frac{3}{8} =$	$5\frac{1}{3} =$	$3\frac{1}{4} =$	$4\frac{1}{2} =$
$1\frac{7}{8} =$	$2\frac{2}{3} =$	$1\frac{5}{8} =$	$3\frac{3}{4} =$	$7\frac{1}{2} =$

Mental Math

a.	b.	c.	d.
e.	f.	g.	h.

Problem Solving

Understand

What information am I given?

What am I asked to find or do?

- -

Plan

How can I use the information I am given?

Which strategy should I try?

- -

Solve

Did I follow the plan?

Did I show my work?

Did I write the answer?

- -

Check

Did I use the correct information?

Did I do what was asked?

Is my answer reasonable?

Facts   Multiply or divide as indicated.

4 × 9	4)16	6 × 8	3)12	5 × 7	4)32	3 × 9	9)81	6 × 2	8)64
9 × 7	8)40	2 × 4	6)42	5 × 5	7)14	7 × 7	8)8	3 × 3	6)0
7 × 3	2)10	10 × 10	3)24	4 × 5	9)54	9 × 1	3)6	7 × 4	7)56
6 × 6	2)18	3 × 5	5)30	2 × 2	6)18	9 × 5	6)24	2 × 8	9)72

Mental Math

a.	**b.**	**c.**	**d.**
e.	**f.**	**g.**	**h.**

Problem Solving

Understand

What information am I given?

What am I asked to find or do?

Plan

How can I use the information I am given?

Which strategy should I try?

Solve

Did I follow the plan?

Did I show my work?

Did I write the answer?

Check

Did I use the correct information?

Did I do what was asked?

Is my answer reasonable?

Facts

Write the abbreviation.	Complete each equivalence.	Complete each conversion.
Metric Units:	Metric Units:	14. 2 liters = _____ milliliters
1. liter _____	7. 1 liter = _____ milliliters	15. 2 liters ≈ _____ quarts
2. milliliter _____	U.S. Customary Units:	16. 3.78 liters = _____ milliliters
U.S. Customary Units:	8. 1 cup = _____ ounces	17. 0.5 liter = _____ milliliters
3. ounces _____	9. 1 pint = _____ ounces	18. $\frac{1}{2}$ gallon = _____ quarts
4. pint _____	10. 1 pint = _____ cups	19. 2 gallons = _____ quarts
5. quart _____	11. 1 quart = _____ pints	20. 2 half gallons = _____ gallon
6. gallon _____	12. 1 gallon = _____ quarts	21. 8 cups = _____ quarts
	Between Systems:	22–23. A two-liter bottle is a little more than _____ quarts or _____ gallon.
	13. 1 liter ≈ _____ quart	

Mental Math

a.	b.	c.	d.
e.	f.	g.	h.

Problem Solving

Understand

What information am I given?
What am I asked to find or do?

Plan

How can I use the information I am given?
Which strategy should I try?

Solve

Did I follow the plan?
Did I show my work?
Did I write the answer?

Check

Did I use the correct information?
Did I do what was asked?
Is my answer reasonable?

Facts Write each improper fraction as a mixed number. Reduce fractions.

$\frac{5}{4} =$	$\frac{6}{4} =$	$\frac{15}{10} =$	$\frac{8}{3} =$	$\frac{15}{12} =$
$\frac{12}{8} =$	$\frac{10}{8} =$	$\frac{3}{2} =$	$\frac{15}{6} =$	$\frac{10}{4} =$
$\frac{8}{6} =$	$\frac{25}{10} =$	$\frac{9}{6} =$	$\frac{10}{6} =$	$\frac{15}{8} =$
$\frac{12}{10} =$	$\frac{10}{3} =$	$\frac{18}{12} =$	$\frac{5}{2} =$	$\frac{4}{3} =$

Mental Math

a.	b.	c.	d.
e.	f.	g.	h.

Problem Solving

Understand
What information am I given?
What am I asked to find or do?

Plan
How can I use the information I am given?
Which strategy should I try?

Solve
Did I follow the plan?
Did I show my work?
Did I write the answer?

Check
Did I use the correct information?
Did I do what was asked?
Is my answer reasonable?

Facts

Complete each equivalent measure.

1. 1 cm = _____ mm
2. 1 m = _____ mm
3. 1 m = _____ cm
4. 1 km = _____ m

5. 1 in. = _____ cm
6. 1 mi ≈ _____ m

7. 1 ft = _____ in.
8. 1 yd = _____ in.
9. 1 yd = _____ ft
10. 1 mi = _____ ft

11. 1 m ≈ _____ in.
12. 1 km ≈ _____ mi

13. 10 cm = _____ mm
14. 2 m = _____ cm
15. 5 km = _____ m
16. 2.5 cm = _____ mm
17. 1.5 m = _____ cm
18. 7.5 km = _____ m

19. $\frac{1}{2}$ ft = _____ in.
20. 2 ft = _____ in.
21. 3 ft = _____ in.
22. 2 yd = _____ ft
23. 10 yd = _____ ft
24. 100 yd = _____ ft

Write a unit for each reference.

Metric Units:

25. The thickness of a dime:
    _____

26. The width of a little finger:
    _____

27. The length of one big step:
    _____

U.S. Customary Units:

28. The width of two fingers:
    _____

29. The length of a man's shoe:
    _____

30. The length of one big step:
    _____

Mental Math

a.	b.	c.	d.
e.	f.	g.	h.

Problem Solving

Understand

What information am I given?
What am I asked to find or do?

Plan

How can I use the information I am given?
Which strategy should I try?

Solve

Did I follow the plan?
Did I show my work?
Did I write the answer?

Check

Did I use the correct information?
Did I do what was asked?
Is my answer reasonable?

Facts   Reduce each fraction to lowest terms.

$\frac{2}{8} =$	$\frac{4}{6} =$	$\frac{6}{10} =$	$\frac{2}{4} =$	$\frac{5}{100} =$	$\frac{9}{12} =$
$\frac{4}{10} =$	$\frac{4}{12} =$	$\frac{2}{10} =$	$\frac{3}{6} =$	$\frac{25}{100} =$	$\frac{3}{12} =$
$\frac{4}{16} =$	$\frac{3}{9} =$	$\frac{6}{9} =$	$\frac{4}{8} =$	$\frac{2}{12} =$	$\frac{6}{12} =$
$\frac{8}{16} =$	$\frac{2}{6} =$	$\frac{8}{12} =$	$\frac{6}{8} =$	$\frac{5}{10} =$	$\frac{75}{100} =$

Mental Math

a.	**b.**	**c.**	**d.**
e.	**f.**	**g.**	**h.**

Problem Solving

Understand
What information am I given?
What am I asked to find or do?

- -

Plan
How can I use the information I am given?
Which strategy should I try?

- -

Solve
Did I follow the plan?
Did I show my work?
Did I write the answer?

- -

Check
Did I use the correct information?
Did I do what was asked?
Is my answer reasonable?

Name _____ Time _____

Facts   Multiply.

7 × 7	4 × 6	8 × 1	2 × 2	0 × 5	6 × 3	8 × 9	5 × 8	6 × 2	10 × 10
9 × 4	2 × 5	9 × 6	7 × 3	5 × 5	7 × 2	6 × 8	3 × 5	9 × 9	5 × 4
3 × 4	6 × 5	8 × 2	4 × 4	6 × 7	8 × 8	2 × 3	7 × 4	5 × 9	3 × 8
3 × 9	7 × 8	2 × 4	5 × 7	3 × 3	9 × 7	4 × 8	0 × 0	9 × 2	6 × 6

Mental Math

a.	b.	c.	d.
e.	f.	g.	h.

Problem Solving

Understand

What information am I given?
What am I asked to find or do?

- -

Plan

How can I use the information I am given?
Which strategy should I try?

- -

Solve

Did I follow the plan?
Did I show my work?
Did I write the answer?

- -

Check

Did I use the correct information?
Did I do what was asked?
Is my answer reasonable?

Facts

Write the abbreviation.	Complete each equivalence.	Complete each conversion.
Metric Units:	Metric Units:	14. 2 liters = _____ milliliters
1. liter _____	7. 1 liter = _____ milliliters	15. 2 liters ≈ _____ quarts
2. milliliter _____	U.S. Customary Units:	16. 3.78 liters = _____ milliliters
U.S. Customary Units:	8. 1 cup = _____ ounces	17. 0.5 liter = _____ milliliters
3. ounces _____	9. 1 pint = _____ ounces	18. $\frac{1}{2}$ gallon = _____ quarts
4. pint _____	10. 1 pint = _____ cups	19. 2 gallons = _____ quarts
5. quart _____	11. 1 quart = _____ pints	20. 2 half gallons = _____ gallon
6. gallon _____	12. 1 gallon = _____ quarts	21. 8 cups = _____ quarts
	Between Systems:	22–23. A two-liter bottle is a little more than _____ quarts or _____ gallon.
	13. 1 liter ≈ _____ quart	

Mental Math

a.	b.	c.	d.
e.	f.	g.	h.

Problem Solving

Understand
What information am I given?
What am I asked to find or do?

- -

Plan
How can I use the information I am given?
Which strategy should I try?

- -

Solve
Did I follow the plan?
Did I show my work?
Did I write the answer?

- -

Check
Did I use the correct information?
Did I do what was asked?
Is my answer reasonable?

| Facts | Write each mixed number as an improper fraction. |

$2\frac{1}{2} =$	$2\frac{2}{5} =$	$1\frac{3}{4} =$	$2\frac{3}{4} =$	$2\frac{1}{8} =$
$1\frac{2}{3} =$	$3\frac{1}{2} =$	$1\frac{5}{6} =$	$2\frac{1}{4} =$	$1\frac{1}{8} =$
$5\frac{1}{2} =$	$1\frac{3}{8} =$	$5\frac{1}{3} =$	$3\frac{1}{4} =$	$4\frac{1}{2} =$
$1\frac{7}{8} =$	$2\frac{2}{3} =$	$1\frac{5}{8} =$	$3\frac{3}{4} =$	$7\frac{1}{2} =$

Mental Math

a.	**b.**	**c.**	**d.**
e.	**f.**	**g.**	**h.**

Problem Solving

Understand

What information am I given?

What am I asked to find or do?

Plan

How can I use the information I am given?

Which strategy should I try?

Solve

Did I follow the plan?

Did I show my work?

Did I write the answer?

Check

Did I use the correct information?

Did I do what was asked?

Is my answer reasonable?

Name _____ Time _____

Facts

Complete each equivalent measure.		Write a unit for each reference.

Complete each equivalent measure.

1. 1 cm = _____ mm
2. 1 m = _____ mm
3. 1 m = _____ cm
4. 1 km = _____ m

5. 1 in. = _____ cm
6. 1 mi ≈ _____ m

7. 1 ft = _____ in.
8. 1 yd = _____ in.
9. 1 yd = _____ ft
10. 1 mi = _____ ft

11. 1 m ≈ _____ in.
12. 1 km ≈ _____ mi

13. 10 cm = _____ mm
14. 2 m = _____ cm
15. 5 km = _____ m
16. 2.5 cm = _____ mm
17. 1.5 m = _____ cm
18. 7.5 km = _____ m

19. $\frac{1}{2}$ ft = _____ in.
20. 2 ft = _____ in.
21. 3 ft = _____ in.
22. 2 yd = _____ ft
23. 10 yd = _____ ft
24. 100 yd = _____ ft

Write a unit for each reference.

Metric Units:

25. The thickness of a dime:
_____

26. The width of a little finger:
_____

27. The length of one big step:
_____

U.S. Customary Units:

28. The width of two fingers:
_____

29. The length of a man's shoe:
_____

30. The length of one big step:
_____

Mental Math

a.	b.	c.	d.
e.	f.	g.	h.

Problem Solving

Understand
What information am I given?
What am I asked to find or do?

- -

Plan
How can I use the information I am given?
Which strategy should I try?

- -

Solve
Did I follow the plan?
Did I show my work?
Did I write the answer?

- -

Check
Did I use the correct information?
Did I do what was asked?
Is my answer reasonable?

Facts   Write each improper fraction as a mixed number. Reduce fractions.

$\frac{5}{4} =$	$\frac{6}{4} =$	$\frac{15}{10} =$	$\frac{8}{3} =$	$\frac{15}{12} =$
$\frac{12}{8} =$	$\frac{10}{8} =$	$\frac{3}{2} =$	$\frac{15}{6} =$	$\frac{10}{4} =$
$\frac{8}{6} =$	$\frac{25}{10} =$	$\frac{9}{6} =$	$\frac{10}{6} =$	$\frac{15}{8} =$
$\frac{12}{10} =$	$\frac{10}{3} =$	$\frac{18}{12} =$	$\frac{5}{2} =$	$\frac{4}{3} =$

Mental Math

a.	b.	c.	d.
e.	f.	g.	h.

Problem Solving

Understand

What information am I given?
What am I asked to find or do?

- -

Plan

How can I use the information I am given?
Which strategy should I try?

- -

Solve

Did I follow the plan?
Did I show my work?
Did I write the answer?

- -

Check

Did I use the correct information?
Did I do what was asked?
Is my answer reasonable?

Facts   Multiply or divide as indicated.

4 $\times 9$	$4\overline{)16}$	6 $\times 8$	$3\overline{)12}$	5 $\times 7$	$4\overline{)32}$	3 $\times 9$	$9\overline{)81}$	6 $\times 2$	$8\overline{)64}$
9 $\times 7$	$8\overline{)40}$	2 $\times 4$	$6\overline{)42}$	5 $\times 5$	$7\overline{)14}$	7 $\times 7$	$8\overline{)8}$	3 $\times 3$	$6\overline{)0}$
7 $\times 3$	$2\overline{)10}$	10 $\times 10$	$3\overline{)24}$	4 $\times 5$	$9\overline{)54}$	9 $\times 1$	$3\overline{)6}$	7 $\times 4$	$7\overline{)56}$
6 $\times 6$	$2\overline{)18}$	3 $\times 5$	$5\overline{)30}$	2 $\times 2$	$6\overline{)18}$	9 $\times 5$	$6\overline{)24}$	2 $\times 8$	$9\overline{)72}$

Mental Math

a.	b.	c.	d.
e.	f.	g.	h.

Problem Solving

Understand
What information am I given?
What am I asked to find or do?

Plan
How can I use the information I am given?
Which strategy should I try?

Solve
Did I follow the plan?
Did I show my work?
Did I write the answer?

Check
Did I use the correct information?
Did I do what was asked?
Is my answer reasonable?

Facts   Write each percent as a reduced fraction and decimal number.

Percent	Fraction	Decimal	Percent	Fraction	Decimal
5%			10%		
20%			30%		
25%			50%		
1%			$12\frac{1}{2}$%		
90%			$33\frac{1}{3}$%		
75%			$66\frac{2}{3}$%		

Mental Math

a.	b.	c.	d.
e.	f.	g.	h.

Problem Solving

Understand

What information am I given?

What am I asked to find or do?

Plan

How can I use the information I am given?

Which strategy should I try?

Solve

Did I follow the plan?

Did I show my work?

Did I write the answer?

Check

Did I use the correct information?

Did I do what was asked?

Is my answer reasonable?

Saxon Math Course 1

Name _____ Time _____

Facts Write each percent as a reduced fraction and decimal number.

Percent	Fraction	Decimal	Percent	Fraction	Decimal
5%			10%		
20%			30%		
25%			50%		
1%			$12\frac{1}{2}$%		
90%			$33\frac{1}{3}$%		
75%			$66\frac{2}{3}$%		

Mental Math

a.	b.	c.	d.
e.	f.	g.	h.

Problem Solving

Understand

What information am I given?

What am I asked to find or do?

- -

Plan

How can I use the information I am given?

Which strategy should I try?

- -

Solve

Did I follow the plan?

Did I show my work?

Did I write the answer?

- -

Check

Did I use the correct information?

Did I do what was asked?

Is my answer reasonable?

NOTE: Lesson 104 Power Up has been omitted since the New Concept
will take about half the class period.

Facts Write each percent as a reduced fraction and decimal number.

Percent	Fraction	Decimal	Percent	Fraction	Decimal
5%			10%		
20%			30%		
25%			50%		
1%			$12\frac{1}{2}\%$		
90%			$33\frac{1}{3}\%$		
75%			$66\frac{2}{3}\%$		

Mental Math

a.	b.	c.	d.
e.	f.	g.	h.

Problem Solving

Understand
What information am I given?
What am I asked to find or do?

- -

Plan
How can I use the information I am given?
Which strategy should I try?

- -

Solve
Did I follow the plan?
Did I show my work?
Did I write the answer?

- -

Check
Did I use the correct information?
Did I do what was asked?
Is my answer reasonable?

Facts

Complete each equivalent measure.		Write a unit for each reference.

Complete each equivalent measure.

1. 1 cm = _____ mm
2. 1 m = _____ mm
3. 1 m = _____ cm
4. 1 km = _____ m

5. 1 in. = _____ cm
6. 1 mi ≈ _____ m

7. 1 ft = _____ in.
8. 1 yd = _____ in.
9. 1 yd = _____ ft
10. 1 mi = _____ ft

11. 1 m ≈ _____ in.
12. 1 km ≈ _____ mi

13. 10 cm = _____ mm
14. 2 m = _____ cm
15. 5 km = _____ m
16. 2.5 cm = _____ mm
17. 1.5 m = _____ cm
18. 7.5 km = _____ m

19. $\frac{1}{2}$ ft = _____ in.
20. 2 ft = _____ in.
21. 3 ft = _____ in.
22. 2 yd = _____ ft
23. 10 yd = _____ ft
24. 100 yd = _____ ft

Write a unit for each reference.

Metric Units:

25. The thickness of a dime:
_____

26. The width of a little finger:
_____

27. The length of one big step:
_____

U.S. Customary Units:

28. The width of two fingers:
_____

29. The length of a man's shoe:
_____

30. The length of one big step:
_____

Mental Math

a.	b.	c.	d.
e.	f.	g.	h.

Problem Solving

Understand

What information am I given?
What am I asked to find or do?

Plan

How can I use the information I am given?
Which strategy should I try?

Solve

Did I follow the plan?
Did I show my work?
Did I write the answer?

Check

Did I use the correct information?
Did I do what was asked?
Is my answer reasonable?

Facts   Write each percent as a reduced fraction and decimal number.

Percent	Fraction	Decimal	Percent	Fraction	Decimal
5%			10%		
20%			30%		
25%			50%		
1%			$12\frac{1}{2}\%$		
90%			$33\frac{1}{3}\%$		
75%			$66\frac{2}{3}\%$		

Mental Math

a.	b.	c.	d.
e.	f.	g.	h.

Problem Solving

Understand

What information am I given?

What am I asked to find or do?

- -

Plan

How can I use the information I am given?

Which strategy should I try?

- -

Solve

Did I follow the plan?

Did I show my work?

Did I write the answer?

- -

Check

Did I use the correct information?

Did I do what was asked?

Is my answer reasonable?

Facts Write each percent as a reduced fraction and decimal number.

Percent	Fraction	Decimal	Percent	Fraction	Decimal
5%			10%		
20%			30%		
25%			50%		
1%			$12\frac{1}{2}\%$		
90%			$33\frac{1}{3}\%$		
75%			$66\frac{2}{3}\%$		

Mental Math

a.	b.	c.	d.
e.	f.	g.	h.

Problem Solving

Understand

What information am I given?

What am I asked to find or do?

- -

Plan

How can I use the information I am given?

Which strategy should I try?

- -

Solve

Did I follow the plan?

Did I show my work?

Did I write the answer?

- -

Check

Did I use the correct information?

Did I do what was asked?

Is my answer reasonable?

Facts   Complete each equivalence.

1. Draw a segment about 1 cm long.

2. Draw a segment about 1 inch long.

3. One inch is how many centimeters? _____

4. Which is longer, 1 km or 1 mi? _____

5. Which is longer, 1 km or $\frac{1}{2}$ mi? _____

6. How many ounces are in a pound? _____

7. How many pounds are in a ton? _____

8. A dollar bill has a mass of about one _____.

9. A pair of shoes has a mass of about one _____.

10. On Earth a kilogram mass weighs about _____ pounds.

11. A metric ton is _____ kilograms.

12. On Earth a metric ton weighs about _____ pounds.

13. The Earth rotates on its axis once in a _____.

14. The Earth revolves around the Sun once in a _____.

15. Water boils

_____ °F

16. _____ °C

17. Normal body temperature

_____ °F

18. _____ °C

19. Cool room temperature

_____ °F

20. _____ °C

21. Water freezes

_____ °F

22. _____ °C

Mental Math

a.	b.	c.	d.
e.	f.	g.	h.

Problem Solving

Understand

What information am I given?

What am I asked to find or do?

Plan

How can I use the information I am given?

Which strategy should I try?

Solve

Did I follow the plan?

Did I show my work?

Did I write the answer?

Check

Did I use the correct information?

Did I do what was asked?

Is my answer reasonable?

Facts   Write each percent as a reduced fraction and decimal number.

Percent	Fraction	Decimal	Percent	Fraction	Decimal
5%			10%		
20%			30%		
25%			50%		
1%			$12\frac{1}{2}$%		
90%			$33\frac{1}{3}$%		
75%			$66\frac{2}{3}$%		

Mental Math

a.	b.	c.	d.
e.	f.	g.	h.

Problem Solving

Understand

What information am I given?

What am I asked to find or do?

- -

Plan

How can I use the information I am given?

Which strategy should I try?

- -

Solve

Did I follow the plan?

Did I show my work?

Did I write the answer?

- -

Check

Did I use the correct information?

Did I do what was asked?

Is my answer reasonable?

Facts   Complete each equivalence.

1. Draw a segment about 1 cm long.

2. Draw a segment about 1 inch long.

3. One inch is how many centimeters? _____

4. Which is longer, 1 km or 1 mi? _____

5. Which is longer, 1 km or $\frac{1}{2}$ mi? _____

6. How many ounces are in a pound? _____

7. How many pounds are in a ton? _____

8. A dollar bill has a mass of about one _____.

9. A pair of shoes has a mass of about one _____.

10. On Earth a kilogram mass weighs about _____ pounds.

11. A metric ton is _____ kilograms.

12. On Earth a metric ton weighs about _____ pounds.

13. The Earth rotates on its axis once in a _____.

14. The Earth revolves around the Sun once in a _____.

15. Water boils
_____ °F

16. _____ °C

17. Normal body temperature
_____ °F

18. _____ °C

19. Cool room temperature
_____ °F

20. _____ °C

21. Water freezes
_____ °F

22. _____ °C

F°   C°

Mental Math

a.	b.	c.	d.
e.	f.	g.	h.

Problem Solving

Understand
What information am I given?
What am I asked to find or do?

- -

Plan
How can I use the information I am given?
Which strategy should I try?

- -

Solve
Did I follow the plan?
Did I show my work?
Did I write the answer?

- -

Check
Did I use the correct information?
Did I do what was asked?
Is my answer reasonable?

Facts   Write each percent as a reduced fraction and decimal number.

Percent	Fraction	Decimal	Percent	Fraction	Decimal
5%			10%		
20%			30%		
25%			50%		
1%			$12\frac{1}{2}\%$		
90%			$33\frac{1}{3}\%$		
75%			$66\frac{2}{3}\%$		

Mental Math

a.	**b.**	**c.**	**d.**
e.	**f.**	**g.**	**h.**

Problem Solving

Understand

What information am I given?

What am I asked to find or do?

- -

Plan

How can I use the information I am given?

Which strategy should I try?

- -

Solve

Did I follow the plan?

Did I show my work?

Did I write the answer?

- -

Check

Did I use the correct information?

Did I do what was asked?

Is my answer reasonable?

© Houghton Mifflin Harcourt Publishing Company and Stephen Hake

Facts Complete each equivalence.

1. Draw a segment about 1 cm long.

2. Draw a segment about 1 inch long.

3. One inch is how many centimeters? _____

4. Which is longer, 1 km or 1 mi? _____

5. Which is longer, 1 km or $\frac{1}{2}$ mi? _____

6. How many ounces are in a pound? _____

7. How many pounds are in a ton? _____

8. A dollar bill has a mass of about one _____.

9. A pair of shoes has a mass of about one _____.

10. On Earth a kilogram mass weighs about _____ pounds.

11. A metric ton is _____ kilograms.

12. On Earth a metric ton weighs about _____ pounds.

13. The Earth rotates on its axis once in a _____.

14. The Earth revolves around the Sun once in a _____.

15. Water boils
_____ °F

16. _____ °C

17. Normal body temperature
_____ °F

18. _____ °C

19. Cool room temperature
_____ °F

20. _____ °C

21. Water freezes
_____ °F

22. _____ °C

Mental Math

a.	b.	c.	d.
e.	f.	g.	h.

Problem Solving

Understand
What information am I given?
What am I asked to find or do?

Plan
How can I use the information I am given?
Which strategy should I try?

Solve
Did I follow the plan?
Did I show my work?
Did I write the answer?

Check
Did I use the correct information?
Did I do what was asked?
Is my answer reasonable?

Facts	Write each percent as a reduced fraction and decimal number.					

Percent	Fraction	Decimal	Percent	Fraction	Decimal
5%			10%		
20%			30%		
25%			50%		
1%			$12\frac{1}{2}\%$		
90%			$33\frac{1}{3}\%$		
75%			$66\frac{2}{3}\%$		

Mental Math

a.	b.	c.	d.
e.	f.	g.	h.

Problem Solving

Understand

What information am I given?
What am I asked to find or do?

- -

Plan

How can I use the information I am given?
Which strategy should I try?

- -

Solve

Did I follow the plan?
Did I show my work?
Did I write the answer?

- -

Check

Did I use the correct information?
Did I do what was asked?
Is my answer reasonable?

Facts Complete each equivalence.

1. Draw a segment about 1 cm long.

2. Draw a segment about 1 inch long.

3. One inch is how many centimeters? _____

4. Which is longer, 1 km or 1 mi? _____

5. Which is longer, 1 km or $\frac{1}{2}$ mi? _____

6. How many ounces are in a pound? _____

7. How many pounds are in a ton? _____

8. A dollar bill has a mass of about one _____.

9. A pair of shoes has a mass of about one _____.

10. On Earth a kilogram mass weighs about _____ pounds.

11. A metric ton is _____ kilograms.

12. On Earth a metric ton weighs about _____ pounds.

13. The Earth rotates on its axis once in a _____.

14. The Earth revolves around the Sun once in a _____.

15. Water boils _____°F

16. _____°C

17. Normal body temperature _____°F

18. _____°C

19. Cool room temperature _____°F

20. _____°C

21. Water freezes _____°F

22. _____°C

Mental Math

a.	b.	c.	d.
e.	f.	g.	h.

Problem Solving

Understand

What information am I given?
What am I asked to find or do?

Plan

How can I use the information I am given?
Which strategy should I try?

Solve

Did I follow the plan?
Did I show my work?
Did I write the answer?

Check

Did I use the correct information?
Did I do what was asked?
Is my answer reasonable?

Facts   Write each percent as a reduced fraction and decimal number.

Percent	Fraction	Decimal	Percent	Fraction	Decimal
5%			10%		
20%			30%		
25%			50%		
1%			$12\frac{1}{2}\%$		
90%			$33\frac{1}{3}\%$		
75%			$66\frac{2}{3}\%$		

Mental Math

a.	b.	c.	d.
e.	f.	g.	h.

Problem Solving

Understand

What information am I given?
What am I asked to find or do?

Plan

How can I use the information I am given?
Which strategy should I try?

Solve

Did I follow the plan?
Did I show my work?
Did I write the answer?

Check

Did I use the correct information?
Did I do what was asked?
Is my answer reasonable?

Facts   Complete each equivalence.

1. Draw a segment about 1 cm long.

2. Draw a segment about 1 inch long.

3. One inch is how many centimeters? _____

4. Which is longer, 1 km or 1 mi? _____

5. Which is longer, 1 km or $\frac{1}{2}$ mi? _____

6. How many ounces are in a pound? _____

7. How many pounds are in a ton? _____

8. A dollar bill has a mass of about one _____.

9. A pair of shoes has a mass of about one _____.

10. On Earth a kilogram mass weighs about _____ pounds.

11. A metric ton is _____ kilograms.

12. On Earth a metric ton weighs about _____ pounds.

13. The Earth rotates on its axis once in a _____.

14. The Earth revolves around the Sun once in a _____.

15. Water boils _____ °F

16. _____ °C

17. Normal body temperature _____ °F

18. _____ °C

19. Cool room temperature _____ °F

20. _____ °C

21. Water freezes _____ °F

22. _____ °C

Mental Math

a.	b.	c.	d.
e.	f.	g.	h.

Problem Solving

Understand
What information am I given?
What am I asked to find or do?

Plan
How can I use the information I am given?
Which strategy should I try?

Solve
Did I follow the plan?
Did I show my work?
Did I write the answer?

Check
Did I use the correct information?
Did I do what was asked?
Is my answer reasonable?

Facts   Write each percent as a reduced fraction and decimal number.

Percent	Fraction	Decimal		Percent	Fraction	Decimal
5%				10%		
20%				30%		
25%				50%		
1%				$12\frac{1}{2}\%$		
90%				$33\frac{1}{3}\%$		
75%				$66\frac{2}{3}\%$		

Mental Math

a.	b.	c.	d.
e.	f.	g.	h.

Problem Solving

Understand

What information am I given?
What am I asked to find or do?

- -

Plan

How can I use the information I am given?
Which strategy should I try?

- -

Solve

Did I follow the plan?
Did I show my work?
Did I write the answer?

- -

Check

Did I use the correct information?
Did I do what was asked?
Is my answer reasonable?

Facts   Complete each equivalence.

1. Draw a segment about 1 cm long.

2. Draw a segment about 1 inch long.

3. One inch is how many centimeters? _____

4. Which is longer, 1 km or 1 mi? _____

5. Which is longer, 1 km or $\frac{1}{2}$ mi? _____

6. How many ounces are in a pound? _____

7. How many pounds are in a ton? _____

8. A dollar bill has a mass of about one _____.

9. A pair of shoes has a mass of about one _____.

10. On Earth a kilogram mass weighs about _____ pounds.

11. A metric ton is _____ kilograms.

12. On Earth a metric ton weighs about _____ pounds.

13. The Earth rotates on its axis once in a _____.

14. The Earth revolves around the Sun once in a _____.

15. Water boils _____ °F

16. _____ °C

17. Normal body temperature _____ °F

18. _____ °C

19. Cool room temperature _____ °F

20. _____ °C

21. Water freezes _____ °F

22. _____ °C

Mental Math

a.	b.	c.	d.
e.	f.	g.	h.

Problem Solving

Understand

What information am I given?

What am I asked to find or do?

Plan

How can I use the information I am given?

Which strategy should I try?

Solve

Did I follow the plan?

Did I show my work?

Did I write the answer?

Check

Did I use the correct information?

Did I do what was asked?

Is my answer reasonable?

Facts   Write each percent as a reduced fraction and decimal number.

Percent	Fraction	Decimal	Percent	Fraction	Decimal
5%			10%		
20%			30%		
25%			50%		
1%			$12\frac{1}{2}$%		
90%			$33\frac{1}{3}$%		
75%			$66\frac{2}{3}$%		

Mental Math

a.	b.	c.	d.
e.	f.	g.	h.

Problem Solving

Understand

What information am I given?

What am I asked to find or do?

- -

Plan

How can I use the information I am given?

Which strategy should I try?

- -

Solve

Did I follow the plan?

Did I show my work?

Did I write the answer?

- -

Check

Did I use the correct information?

Did I do what was asked?

Is my answer reasonable?

© Houghton Mifflin Harcourt Publishing Company and Stephen Hake